Death of Robert Earl of Huntington

by
Anthony Munday

HENRY CHETTLE, who certainly joined Anthony Munday in writing *The Death of Robert Earl of Huntington,** if he did not also assist in penning the *Downfall of Robert Earl of Huntington*, was a very prolific dramatic author. Malone erroneously states, that he was the writer of, or was concerned in, thirty plays: according to information which he himself furnishes, forty-two are, either wholly or in part, to be assigned to Chettle. The titles of only twenty-five are inserted in the *Biographia Dramatica*. The proof of his connection with the historical play now reprinted, has been already supplied,† and it is derived from the same source as nearly all the rest of the intelligence regarding his works—the MSS. of Henslowe.

Of the incidents of the life of Henry Chettle absolutely nothing is known: we are ignorant of the times and places of his birth and death, and of the manner in which he obtained his education. It has been conjectured that he either was, or had been, a printer, but the

---

* Two lines in the Epilogue might be quoted to shew that only one author was concerned in it:

" Thus is Matilda's story shewn in act,
    And rough-hewn out by *an* uncunning hand."

But probably the assertion is not to be taken strictly; or if it be, it will not prove that Chettle had no hand, earlier or later, in the authorship. Mr. Gifford in his Introduction to Ford's Works, Vol. 1. xvi. remarks very truly, that we are not to suppose from the combination of names of authors, " that they were always simultaneously employed in the production of the same play;" and Munday, who was perhaps an elder poet than Chettle, may have himself originally written both parts of *The Earl of Huntington*, the connection of Chettle with them being subsequent, in making alterations or adapting them to the prevailing taste.

† See *The Downfall of Robert Earl of Huntington*, p. 3.

point is very doubtful.* In a tract by him called *England's Mourning Garment*, on the Death of Queen Elizabeth, he speaks of himself as having been "young almost thirty years ago," and as having been a witness of what passed at that period in the Court. If Ritson's conjecture be well founded, he was an author as early as 1578 ;† but perhaps the poetical tract assigned to him under that date was the production of Henry Constable, the initials of both being the same, and the initials only attesting the authorship.

The first account we have of Chettle in connection with the stage, is under date of April 1592,‡ when, according to Henslowe, he was engaged with Dekker in writing a play called *Troilus and Cressida* ; but there is good reason to infer, that if in 1603 he were "young almost thirty years ago," he had written for the theatre before 1592. Besides, in his "Kinde Harte's Dreame," produced about three months after the death of his friend, Robert Greene, on September 3d, 1592, he speaks generally of his connection with the dramatic poets of that day, as if it were not newly formed. Malone supposed, that Shakespeare, with whom Chettle had then recently become acquainted, was alluded to in the same tract. In *England's Mourning Garment*, Chettle addresses a stanza to Shakespeare, and calls him the "silver-tongued Melicert."

Francis Meres, in his often-quoted *Palladis Tamia*, (1598) includes Chettle in a long list of other writers for the stage, as "one of the best for comedy ;" but in earlier works upon the poetry and literature of England, such as Webbe's *Discourse* in 1586, and Puttenham's *Art of English Poesie* in 1589, he is not mentioned.

Henslowe's list of plays, with the authors' names attached, as discovered and printed by Malone, begins only in October 1597 ; and there the first mention of Chet-

---

* See *Restituta*, II. 367. (note.) † Bibl. Poet. 159.
‡ Malone's Shakespeare, by Boswell, III. 331. Probably there is some error in this date, as the preceding entry on the same subject is April 1599. If so, Henslowe's authority on this point does not carry us so far back by five years.

tle is in February 1597-8 : between that date and March
1602-3, a period of little more than five years, he wrote,
or assisted in writing, all the dramatic performances with
which his name is associated; a fact of itself sufficient
to shew, if Henslowe be accurate, that in many of them
his share must have been very inconsiderable, perhaps
only amounting to a few alterations. They are the following, exclusive of those pieces already enumerated,*
in which he was concerned with Munday.

1. The Valiant Welchman, by Michael Drayton and
Henry Chettle, February 1597-8　Printed in 1615. †

2. Earl Goodwin and his three Sons, Part I. by
Michael Drayton, Henry Chettle, Thomas Dekker, and
Robert Wilson, March 1598. Not printed.

3. Earl Goodwin, Part II. by the same authors, and
under the same date in Henslowe's papers. Not printed.

4. Piers of Exton, by the same authors, same date.
Not printed.

5. Black Batman of the North, Part I. by Henry
Chettle, April 1598. Not printed.

6. Black Batman of the North, Part II. by Henry
Chettle and Robert Wilson. Same date. Not printed.

7. The Play of a Woman, by Henry Chettle, July
1598. Not printed.

8. The Conquest of Brute with the first finding of the
Bath, by John Day, Henry Chettle, and John Singer.
Same date. Not printed.

9. Hot Anger soon Cold, by Henry Porter, Henry
Chettle and Ben Jonson, August 1598. Not printed.

10. Catiline's Conspiracy, by Robert Wilson and
Henry Chettle. Same date. Not printed.

11. 'Tis no Deceit to Deceive the Deceiver, by
Henry Chettle, September 1598. Not printed.

12. Æneas' Revenge, with the tragedy of Polyphe-
mus, by Henry Chettle, February 1598-9. Not printed.

13. Agamemnon, by Henry Chettle and Thomas
Dekker, June 1599. Not printed. Malone thought

---

* Introduction to *Downfall of Robert Earl of Huntington*, p. 7.

† With the letters R. A. on the title-page.

that this was the same play as " Troilus and Cressida" before mentioned.

14. The Stepmother's Tragedy, by Henry Chettle, August 1599. Not printed.

15. Patient Grissel, by Thomas Dekker, Henry Chettle, and William Haughton, December 1599. Printed in 1603.

16. The Arcadian Virgin, by Henry Chettle and William Haughton. Same date. Not printed.

17. Damon and Pythias, by Henry Chettle, January 1599-1600. Not printed.

18. The Seven Wise Masters, by Henry Chettle, Thomas Dekker, William Haughton, and John Day, March 1599-1600. Not printed.

19. The Golden Ass and Cupid and Psyche, by Thomas Dekker, John Day, and Henry Chettle, April 1600. Not printed.

20. The Wooing of Death, by Henry Chettle. Same date. Not printed.

21. The Blind Beggar of Bethnal Green, by Henry Chettle and John Day. Same date. Printed in 1659.

22. All is not Gold that Glisters, by Samuel Rowley and Henry Chettle, March 1600. Not printed.

23. Sebastian King of Portugal, by Henry Chettle and Thomas Dekker, April 1601. Not printed.

24. Cardinal Wolsey, Part I. by Henry Chettle, August 1601 Not printed.

25. Cardinal Wolsey, Part II. by Henry Chettle, May 1602. Not printed.

26. The Orphan's Tragedy, by Henry Chettle, September 1601. Not printed.

27. Too Good to be True, by Henry Chettle, Richard Hathwaye, and Wentworth Smith, November 1601. Not printed.

28. Love parts Friendship, by Henry Chettle and Wentworth Smith, May 1602. Not printed.

29. Tobyas, by Henry Chettle. Same date. Not printed.

30. Jeptha, by Henry Chettle. Same date. Not printed.

31. A Danish Tragedy, by Henry Chettle. Same date. Not printed.

32. Femelanco, by Henry Chettle and —— Robinson, September 1602. Not printed.

33. Lady Jane, Part I. by Henry Chettle, Thomas Dekker, Thomas Heywood, Wentworth Smith, and John Webster, November 1602. Not printed.

34. Lady Jane, Part II. by the same authors, Smith excepted. Same date. Not printed.

35. The London Florentine, Part I. by Thomas Heywood and Henry Chettle, December 1602. Not printed.

36. The London Florentine, Part II. by the same authors. Same date. Not printed.

37. The Tragedy of Hoffman, by Henry Chettle. Same date. Printed in 1631.

38. Jane Shore, by Henry Chettle and John Day, March 1602-3. Not printed.

Among the scattered notices in Henslowe's papers is an entry, datedSeptember 3d, 1599, of 40s. advanced to Chettle, Jonson, Dekker, "and other gentlemen," on account of a tragedy they were engaged upon called "Robert the Second, King of Scots.

The interest of the "second part" of *Robert Earl of Huntington* on the whole, is stronger than that of the first part, and some powerful, though not always tasteful, writing gives effect to the situations. The death of Robin Hood takes place as early as the end of the first act, and attention is afterwards directed to the two, otherwise unconnected, plots of the fate of Lady Bruce and her little Son, and of the love of King John for Matilda. Robert Davenport's tragedy of *King John and Matilda*, printed in 1655, goes precisely over the same ground, and with many decided marks of imitation, especially in the conduct of the story. Davenport's production is inferior in most respects to the earlier work of Chettle and Munday.

DRAMATIS PERSONÆ.*

KING RICHARD THE FIRST.
PRINCE JOHN, *afterwards King.*
ROBERT, *Earl of Huntington.*
LITTLE JOHN.
SCATHLOCK.
SCARLET.
FRIAR TUCK.
MUCH, *the Clown.*
BISHOP OF ELY.
CHESTER.
SALISBURY.
LEICESTER.
RICHMOND.
FITZWATER.
YOUNG FITZWATER.
WINCHESTER.
BRUCE.
YOUNG BRUCE.
BOY, *Son of Lady Bruce.*
OXFORD.
HUBERT.
MOWBRAY.
BONVILLE.
PRIOR OF YORK.
JUSTICE WARMAN.
SIR DONCASTER.
MONK OF BURY.
WILL BRAND.
   Maskers, Messenger, Soldiers, &c.
QUEEN MOTHER.
QUEEN.
MATILDA.
LADY BRUCE.
ABBESS OF DUNMOW.

* There is no list of Characters prefixed to the old 4to.

THE DEATH

OF

ROBERT EARL OF HUNTINGTON.

ACT I. SCENE I.

Enter FRIAR TUCK.*

Friar. HOLLA, holla, holla! follow, follow, follow!
[Like noise within.

Now, benedicite!
. What foul absurdity
Folly and foolery
Had like to follow me
I and my mates,
Like addle pates,
Inviting great states
To see our last play,
Are hunting the hay,
With "ho! that way
The goodly hart, ran."
With "follow, Little John!
Much, play the man!"
And I, like a sot,
Have wholly forgot
The course of our plot.
But cross bow lie down,
Come on, friar's gown,
Hood, cover my crown,
And with a low beck,
Prevent a sharp check.
Blithe sit ye all, and wink at our rude cry:
Mind, where we left in Sherwood merrily

---

* *i. e.* Skelton who is supposed by the author to have acted the
part of Friar Tuck, and who, when first he comes on the stage, is
without his gown and hood.

The king, his train, Robin, his yeomen tall,
Gone to the wood to see the fat deer fall.
We left maid Marian busy in the bower,
And pretty Jenny, looking every hour
For their returning from the hunting game,
And therefore seek to set each thing in frame.
Warman all woeful for his sin we left :
Sir Doncaster, whose villainies and theft
You never heard of, but too soon ye shall,
Hurt with the Prior : shame them both befall !
They two will make our mirth be short and small.
But lest I bring ye sorrow ere the time,
Pardon I beg of your well-judging eyne,
And take in part bad prologue, and rude play.
The hunter's halloo ! Tuck must needs away.
      Therefore down weed,
      Bow do the deed
      To make the stag bleed ;
      And if my hand speed,
      Hey for a cry,
      With a throat strain'd high,
      And a loud yall
      At the beast's fall. [*Exit. Halloo within.*

Enter KING, ELY, FITZWATER, SALISBURY, CHES-
TER, PRINCE JOHN, LITTLE JOHN, SCATHLOCK.

King. Where is our mother?
John. Mounted in a stand :
Six fallow deer have died by her hand.
Fitzwater. Three stags I slew.
Ely. Two bucks by me fell down.
Chester. As many died by me.
Salisbury. But I had three.
John. Scathlock, where's Much?
Scathlock. When last I saw him, may it please your
    Grace,
He and the friar footed it apace.
John. Scathlock, no Grace; your fellow and plain
    John.
Little John. I warrant you, Much will be here anon.
John. Think'st thou, Little John, that he must Jenny
    wed ?

Little John. No doubt he must.

John. Then to adorn his head,
We shall have horns good store.

King. God, for thy grace,
How could I miss the stag I had in chase!
Twice did I hit him in the very neck,
When back my arrows flew, as they had smit
On some sure armour. Where is Robin Hood,
And the wight* Scarlet? Seek them Little John.

                    [Exit Little John.

I'll have that stag before I dine to-day.

            Enter MUCH.

Much. Oh! the friar, the friar, the friar!

King. Why how now Much?

Much. Cry ye mercy, master King:† marry, this is the
matter. Scarlet is following the stag you hit, and has
almost lodged him : now, the Friar has the best bow, but
yours, in all the field ; which, and Scarlet had, he would
have him straight.

King. Where is thy master?

Much. Nay, I cannot tell, nor the Friar neither.

Scathlock. I hear them halloo, far off in the wood.

King. Come, Much, can'st lead us where as Scarlet is?

Much. Never fear you: follow me.

                    [Exeunt hallooing.

SCENE II.

Enter Sir DONCASTER, PRIOR.

Doncaster. You were resolv'd to have him poisoned,
Or kill'd, or made away you car'd not how:
What devil makes you doubtful now to do't?

Prior. Why, Doncaster, his kindness in our needs.

Doncaster. A plague upon his kindness! let him die.
I never temper'd poison in my life,
But I employ'd it. By th' mass, and I lose this,
For ever look to lose my company.

Prior. But will you give it him?

---

   * Wight means *active* or sometimes *clever.* It may be matter of
conjecture whether " *white* boy," " *white* poet," " *white* villain, " &c.
so often found in old dramatists, have not this origin.

   † It is very obvious that Much begins his answer at " Cry ye
mercy, master king," but his name is omitted in the old 4to.

Doncaster. That cannot be.
The Queen, Earl Chester, and Earl Salisbury,
If they once see me, I am a dead man:
Or did they hear my name, I'll lay my life,
They all would hunt me for my life.
   Prior. What hast thou done to them?
   Doncaster. Faith, some odd toys,
That made me fly the south: but pass we them.
Here is the poison; will you give it Robin?
   Prior. Now, by this gold, I will.
   Doncaster. Or, as I said,
For ever I'll defy your company.
   Prior. Well he shall die, and in his jollity:
And in my head I have a policy,
To make him die disgrac'd.
   Doncaster. Oh, tell it, prior!
   Prior. I will, but not as now; [*Call the friar wihin.*
We'll seek a place: the woods have many ears,
And some, methinks, are calling for the friar.*
Enter LITTLE JOHN *and* SCATHLOCK, *calling the Friar
as before.*
   Little John. The friar! the friar!
   Scathlock. Why, where's this friar?
               Enter FRIAR TUCK.
   Friar. Here, sir: what is your desire?
         Enter ROBIN HOOD, *and* WARMAN.†
   Robin. Why Friar, what, a murrain, dost thou mean?
The king calls for thee; for a mighty stag,
(That hath a copper ring about his neck
With letters on it, which he would have read)
Hath Scarlet kill'd. I pray thee go thy way.
   Friar. Master, I will: no longer will I stay.
         [*Exit Friar Tuck, Little John, and Scathlock.*
   Robin. Good uncle, be more careful of your health;
And yours, Sir Doncaster, your wounds are green.

* The old copy adds here *exeunt*, and a new scene is marked; but
this is a mistake, as Robin Hood just afterwards converses with the
Prior, Sir Doncaster, and Warman, without any new entrance on their
part. They retire to the back of the stage.
   † Warman is not mentioned, but we find him on the stage just
afterwards, and he probably enters with Robin Hood. The entrance
of Friar Tuck is also omitted.

Both. Through your great kindness we are comforted.

Robin. And, Warman, I advise you to more mirth.
Shun solitary walks, keep company:
Forget your fault; I have forgiv'n the fault.
Good Warman, be more blithe, and at this time,
A little help my Marian and her maid.
Much shall come to you straight: a little now;
We must all strive to do the best we may.

         [*Exit winding.* *

Warman. On you and her I'll wait until my dying day.

   [*Warman is going out; Doncaster pulls him.*

Doncaster. Warman, a word. My good Lord Prior
  and I
Are full of grief to see thy misery.

Warman. My misery, Sir Doncaster? why, I thank
  God,
I never was in better state than now.

Prior. Why, what a servile slavish mind hast thou!
Art thou a man, and canst be such a beast,
Ass-like, to bear the burthen of thy wrongs?

Warman. What wrong have I? is't wrong to be
  reliev'd?

Doncaster. Reliev'd say'st thou? why, shallow-witted
  fool,
Dost thou not see Robin's ambitious pride,
And how he climbs by pitying, and aspires
By humble looks, good deeds, and such fond toys,
To be a monarch reigning over us,
As if we were the vassals to his will?

Warman. I am his vassal, and I will be still.

Prior. Warman, thou art a fool. I do confess,
Were these good deeds done in sincerity,
Pity of mine, thine† or this knight's distress,
Without vain brags, it were true charity:
But to relieve our fainting body's wants,
And grieve our souls with quips, and bitter 'braids,
Is good turns overturn'd: no thanks we owe
To any, whatsoever helps us so.

    * i. e. winding his horn.
  † The 4to. reads " Pity of *mind,* thine," &c.

Warman. Neither himself nor any that he keeps,
Ever ubpraided me, since I came last.

Doncaster. Oh God, have mercy on thee, silly ass!
Doth he not say to every guest that comes,
This same is Warman, that was once my steward?

Warman. And what of that?

Prior. Is't not as much to say,
Why, here he stands that once did me betray?

Doncaster. Did he not bring a troop to grace himself,
Like captives waiting on a conqueror's chair,
And calling of them out by one and one,
Presented them, like fairings, to the king?*

Prior. Oh, I: there was a rare invention.
A plague upon the fool!
I hate him worse for that than all the rest.

Warman. Why should you hate him? why should you, or. you,
Envy this noble lord thus, as you do?

Doncaster. Nay rather, why dost thou not join in hate
With us, that lately liv'd, like us, in wealthy state?
Remember this, remember, foolish man,
How thou hast been the shrieve of Nottingham.

Prior. Cry to thy thoughts, let this thought never
cease,
" I have been justice of my sovereign's peace,
Lord of fair livings; men with cap and knee,
In liveries waited hourly on me."

Doncaster. And when thou think'st, thou hast been
such and such,
Think, then, what 'tis to be a mate to Much?
To run when Robin bids, come at his call,
Be mistress Marian's man.

Prior. Nay think withal—

Warman. What shall I think, but think upon my need,
When men fed dogs, and me they would not feed?
When I despair'd through want, and sought to die
My piteous master of his charity
Forgave my fault, reliev'd and saved me.
This do I think upon; and you should think

* See the last scene of the first part of this play.

(If you had hope of soul's salvation)
First, Prior, that he is of thy flesh and blood,
That thou art uncle unto Robin Hood;
That by extortion thou did'st get his lands:
God and I know how it came to thy hands.
How thou pursued'st him in his misery,
And how heaven plagued thy heart's extremity.
Think, Doncaster, when hired by this Prior,
Thou cam'st to take my master with the Friar,
And wert thyself ta'en, how he set thee free,
Gave the an hundred pound to comfort thee.
And both bethink ye how, but yesterday
Wounded and naked in the field you lay;
How with his own hand he did raise your heads,
Pour'd balm into your wounds, your bodies fed,
Watch'd when ye slept, wept when he saw your woe—
   Doncaster. Stay, Warman, stay! I grant that he
      did so;
And you, turn'd honest, have forsworn the villain?
   Warman. Even from my soul I villainy defy.
   Prior. A blessed hour: a fit time now to die.
   Doncaster. And you shall, conscience.
                 [*Stab him, Warman falls.*
   Warman. Oh, forgive me, God,
And save my master from their bloody hands!
   Prior. What, hast thou made him sure?
   Doncaster. It's dead sure he's dead, if that be sure.
   Prior. Then let us thrust the dagger in his hand;
And, when the next comes, cry he kill'd himself.
   Doncaster. That must he now: yonder comes Robin
      Hood.

           Enter ROBIN HOOD.

No life in him?
   Prior. No, no, not any life.
Three mortal wounds have let in piercing air,
And at their gaps his life is clean let out.
   Robin. Who is it, uncle, that you so bemoan?
   Prior. Warman, good nephew; whom Sir Doncaster
      and I
Found freshly bleeding, as he now doth lie.

You were scarce gone, when he did stab himself.
   Robin. Oh God!
He in his own hand holds his own heart's hurt:
I dreaded, too, much his distressed look.
Belike the wretch despair'd and slew himself.
   Doncaster. Nay that's most sure : yet he had little
     reason,
Considering how well you used him.
   Robin. Well, I am sorry, but must not be 'sad,
Because the king is coming to my bower.
Help me, I pray thee, to remove his body
Lest he should come and see him murdered.
Some time anon he shall be buried.
   [*Exeunt Robin Hood and Sir Doncaster with the body.**
   Prior. Good! all is good! this is as I desire :
Now for a face of pure hypocrisy.
Sweet murder, clothe thee in religious weeds,
Reign in my bosom, that with help of thee,
I may effect this Robin's tragedy.
     Enter ROBIN HOOD *and* Sir DONCASTER.
   Doncaster. Nay, nay, you must not take this thing so
     heavily.
   Robin. A body's loss, Sir Doncaster, is much ;
But a soul's too, is more to be bemoan'd.
   Prior. Truly, I wonder at your virtuous mind.
Oh, God, to one so kind who'd be unkind !
Let go this grief: now must you put on joy,
And for the many favours I have found,
So much exceeding all conceit of mine,
Unto your cheer I'll add a precious drink,
Of colour rich and red, sent me from Rome.
There's in it Moly,† Syrian Balsamum,

---

* The 4to merely reads *exit.*

† " And yet more medicinal is it than that Moly
   That Hermes once to wise Ulysses gave."
                    MILTON'S COMUS.
There are several kinds of Moly, and one of them distinguished
among horticulturists as Homer's Moly. Sir T. Brown thus quaintly
renders two lines in the Odyssey relating to it:—
   " The Gods it Moly call, whose root to dig away
   Is dangerous unto man, but Gods they all things may."

Gold's rich elixir; Oh, 'tis precious!

Robin. Where is it, uncle?

Prior. As yesterday
Sir Doncaster and I rid on our way,
Thieves did beset us, bound us as you saw:
And among other things did take from me
This rich confection: but regardlessly,
As common drink, they cast into a bush
The bottle, which this day Sir Doncaster
Fetch'd, and hath left it in the inner lodging.
I tell you cousin, (I do love you well).
A pint of this ransom'd the Sophy's son
When he was taken in Natolia.
I meant, indeed, to give it my liege lord,
In hope to have his favour; but to you
I put myself: be my good friend,
And, in your own restoring, me restore.

Robin. Uncle, I will; you need urge that no more.
But what's the virtue of this precious drink?

Prior. It keeps fresh youth, restores diseased sight,
Helps nature's weakness, smooths the scars of wounds,
And cools the entrails with a balmy breath,
When they, by thirst or travel, boil with heat.

Robin. Uncle, I thank you: pray you let me have
A cup prepared 'gainst the king comes in,
To cool his heat: myself will give it him.

Prior. And when he drinks, be bold to say, he drinks
A richer draught than that dissolved pearl,
Which Cleopatra drank to Anthony.

Robin. I have much business: let it be your charge,
To make this rich draught ready for the king,
And I will quite it: pray ye do not fail.   [*Exit.*

Prior. I warrant you, good nephew.

Doncaster. Better, and better still!
We thought before but to have poison'd him,
And now shall Robin Hood destroy the king.
Even when the king, the queen, the prince, the lords,
Joy in his virtues, this supposed vice
Will turn to sharp hate their exceeding love.

Prior. Ha, ha, ha! I cannot chuse but laugh,

c

To see my cousin cozen'd in this sort.
Fail him, quoth you; nay, hang me if I do.
But, Doncaster, art sure the poisons are well mix'd?
  Doncaster. Tut, tut, let me alone for the poisoning:
I have already turn'd o'er four or five
That anger'd me.   But tell me, prior,
Wherefore so deadly dost thou hate thy cousin?
  Prior. Shall I be plain? because, if he were dead,
I should be made the Earl of Huntington.
  Doncaster. A pretty cause: but thou a churchman art.
  Prior. Tut, man, if that would fall,
I'll have a dispensation, and turn temporal.
But tell me, Doncaster, why dost thou hate him?
  Doncaster. By the mass I cannot tell.   Oh, yes, now
      I ha't:
I hate thy cousin Earl of Huntington,
Because so many love him as there do,
And I myself am loved of so few.
Nay, I have other reasons for my hate:
He is a fool and will be reconcil'd,
To any foe he hath: he is too mild,
Too honest for this world, fitter for heaven.
He will not kill these greedy cormorants,
Nor strip base peasants of the wealth they have:
He does abuse a thief's name and an outlaw's,
And is, indeed, no outlaw, nor no thief:
He is unworthy of such reverend names.
Besides, he keeps a paltry whindling girl,
And will not bed, forsooth, before he bride.
I'll stand to't, he abuses maidenhead
That will not take it, being offered,
Hinders the commonwealth of able men.
Another thing I hate him for again:
He says his prayers, fasts eves, gives alms, does good:
For these, and such like crimes, swears Doncaster
To work the speedy death of Robin Hood.
  Prior. Well said, i'faith. Hark, hark! the king
      returns.
To do this deed my heart like fuel burns.   [*Exeunt.*

Wind horns.   Enter KING, QUEEN, JOHN, FITZ-
WATER, ELY, CHESTER, SALISBURY, LEICESTER,
LITTLE JOHN, FRIAR TUCK, SCARLET, SCATH-
LOCK, *and* MUCH : *Friar Tuck carrying a stag's head,
dancing.*

King. Gramercy, Friar, for thy glee,
Thou greatly hast contented me :
What with thy sporting and thy game,
I swear, I highly pleased am.

Friar. It was my master's whole desire
That maiden, yeoman, swain and friar,
Their arts and wits should all apply,
For pleasure of your majesty.

Queen. Son Richard, look, I pray you, on the ring,
That was about the neck of the last stag.

Chester. Was his name Scarlet, that shot off his neck ?

John. Chester, it was this honest fellow Scarlet :
This is the fellow, and a yeoman bold,
As ever cours'd the swift hart on the mould.

King. Friar, here's somewhat grav'd upon the ring;
I pray thee read it : mean while list to me.
    [*This while most compassing the Friar about the ring.*
Scarlet and Scathlock, you bold brethren,
Twelve pence a day I give each for his fee ;
And henceforth see ye live like honest men.

Both. We will, my liege, else let us die the death.

Much. A boon, a boon, upon my knee,
Good King Richard, I beg of thee !
For indeed, sir, the troth is, Much is my father, and he
is one of your tenants, in King's Mill at Wakefield, all
on a green ;
            O there dwelleth a jolly pinder,
            At Wakefield all on a green.*
Now I would have you, if you will do so much for me,

---

* These two lines are taken, with a slight change, from the ballad of
" the Jolly Pinder of Wakefield."   See Ritson's Robin Hood. ii. 16.
            " In Wakefield there lives a jolly pinder,
        In Wakefield all on a green," &c.

to set me forward in the way of marriage to Jenny: the
mill would not be cast away upon us.

King. Much, be thou ever master of that mill:
I give it thee for thine inheritance.

Much. Thanks, precious prince of courtesy.
I'll to Jenny and tell her of my lands, i'faith.   [*Exit.*

John. Here, Friar, here; here it begins.

Friar. (reads) " When Harold hare-foot reigned king,
          About my neck he put this ring."

King. In Harold's time? more than a hundred year
Hath this ring been about this new-slain deer!
I am sorry now it died; but let the same
Head, ring and all, be sent to Nottingham,
And in the castle kept for monuments.

Fitzwater. My liege, I heard an old tale long ago,
That Harold, being Goodwin's son, of Kent,*
When he had got fair England's government,
Hunted for pleasure once within this wood,
And singled out a fair and stately stag,
Which foot to foot the king in running caught:
And sure this was the stag.

King. It was, no doubt.

Chester. But some, my lord, affirm,
That Julius Cæsar, many years before,
Took such a stag, and such a poesy writ.

King. It should not be in Julius Cæsar's time.
There was no English used in this land,
Until the Saxons came; and this is writ
In Saxon characters.

John. Well, 'twas a goodly beast.
          Enter ROBIN HOOD.

King. How now, Earl Robert?

Friar. A forfeit, a forfeit, my liege Lord!
My master's laws are on record:
The court-roll here your Grace may see.

---

* Ritson (notes and illustrations to Robin Hood, i. lxii) observes correctly, that Fitzwater confounds one man with another, and
that Harold Harefoot was the son and successor of Canute the Great.

King. I pray thee, Friar, read them me.

Friar. One shall suffice, and this is he.
No man, that cometh in this wood
To feast or dwell with Robin Hood,
Shall call him Earl, Lord, Knight or Squire :
He no such titles doth desire,
But Robin Hood, plain Robin Hood,
That honest yeoman, stout and good,
On pain of forfeiting a mark,
That must be paid to me his clerk.
My liege, my liege, this law you broke,
Almost in the last word you spoke :
That crime may not acquitted be,
Till Friar Tuck receive his fee.

King. There's more than twenty marks, mad Friar.

                             [Casts him purse.

Friar. If thus you pay the clerk his hire,
Oft may you forfeit, I desire.
You are a perfect penitent,
And well you do your wrong repent :
For this your Highness' liberal gift
I here absolve you, without shrift.

King. Gramercies, friar. Now, Robin Hood,
Sith Robin Hood it needs must be,
I was about to ask before,
If thou didst see the great stag's fall.

Robin. I did, my Lord, I saw it all ;
But missing this same prating friar,
And hearing you so much desire
To have the lozel's company,
I went to seek small honesty.

Friar. But you found much, when you found me.

Robin. I, Much my man ; but not a jot
Of honesty in thee, God wot.

Queen. Robin, you do abuse the Friar.

Friar. Madam, I dare not call him liar :
He may be bold with me he knows.
How now, Prince John, how goes, how goes
This woodman's life with you to-day ?
My fellow Woodnet you would be.

John. I am thy fellow, thou dost see;
And to be plain, as God me save,
So well I like thee, merry knave,
That I thy company must have:
Nay, and I will.
Friar. Nay, and you shall.
Robin. My Lord, you need not fear at all,
But you shall have his company :
He will be bold I warrant you.
King. Know you where e'er a spring is nigh ?
Fain would I drink, I am right dry.
Robin. I have a drink within my bower
Of pleasant taste and sovereign power:
My reverend uncle gives it me,
To give unto your Majesty.
King. I would be loth, indeed, being in heat
To drink cold water.   Let us to thy bower.
Robin. Run, Friar, before,
And bid my uncle be in readiness.
Friar. Gone with a trice* on such good business.

        [Exeunt omnes.

SCENE III.†

Enter MARIAN, *with a white apron.*

Marian. What Much ? What Jenny ? Much, I say !
Much. What's the matter mistress ?
Marian. I pray thee see the fueller
Suffer the cook to want no wood.
Good Lord, where is this idle girl ?
Why Jenny !
Jenny. (within.) I come, forsooth.
Marian. I pray thee, bring the flowers forth.

----

* " *In* a trice" is the usual expression. See a variety of instances
collected by Mr. Todd in his Dictionary, but none of them have it
" *with* a trice," as in this place : the old copy prints the ordi-
nary abbreviation for *with*, which may have been misread by the
printer.

 † The scenes are marked, though incorrectly, in the old copy thus
far ; but the rest of the play is only divided by the *exits* or *entrances*
of the characters.

Much. I'll go send her, mistress ; and help the cooks,
if they have any need.

Marian. Dispatch good Much. What Jen, I say!

Enter JENNY.

Much. Hie ye, hie ye ! she calls for life. [*Exit Much.*

Marian. Indeed, indeed, you do me wrong,
To let me cry, and call so long.

Jenny. Forsooth, I straw'd* the dining bowers,
And smooth'd the walks with herbs and flowers.
The yeomen's tables I have spread,
Dress'd salts, laid trenchers, set on bread.
Nay, all is well, I warrant you.

Marian. You are not well, I promise you,
Your 'foresleeves are not pinn'd ; fie, fie!
And all your head-geer stands awry.
Give me the flowers. Go in, for shame,
And quickly see you mend the same.   [*Exit Jenny.*

Enter SIR DONCASTER, PRIOR. MARIAN *strewing
flowers.*

Doncaster. How busy mistress Marian is :
She thinks this is her day of bliss.

Prior. But it shall be the woeful'st day
That ever chanc'd her, if I may.

Marian. Why are you two thus in the air ?
Your wounds are green. Good coz have care.

Prior. Thanks for your kindness, gentle maid :
My cousin Robert us hath prayed,
To help him in this business.

Enter FRIAR.

Friar. Sir Doncaster, Sir Doncaster !

Doncaster. Holla.

Friar. I pray you did you see the Prior?

Prior. Why here I am. What wouldst thou, Friar?

Friar. The King is heated in the chace,
And posteth hitherward apace.
He told my master he was dry,
And he desires ye, presently,

---

   * Jenny, a country wench, uses the old word *straw'd*; but when
the author speaks afterwards in the stage direction, he describes
Marian as " *strewing* flowers." Shakespeare has *o'er-strawed* in
Venus and Adonis, perhaps for the sake of the rhime.

To send the drink whereof ye spake.

 Prior. Come, it is here : haste let us make.

  [*Exeunt Doncaster, Prior and Friar.   Horns blow.*
Enter KING, QUEEN, JOHN, SCARLET, SCATHLOCK,
  ELY, FITZWATER, SALISBURY, CHESTER. *Marian*
  kneels down.

 Marian. Most gracious Sovereign, welcome once
  again :
Welcome to you, and all your princely train.

 King. Thanks, lovely hostess ; we are homely guests.
Where's Robin Hood ? he promis'd me some drink.

 Marian. Your handmaid, Robin, will not then be long:
The Friar, indeed, came running to his uncle,
Who, with Sir Doncaster, were here with me,
And all together went for such a drink.

 King. Well, in a better time it could not come,
For I am very hot, and passing dry.

 Enter ROBIN HOOD, *a cup, a towel, leading* DONCAS-
  TER : TUCK *and* MUCH *pulling the Prior.*

 Robin. Traitor! I'll draw thee out before the King.

 Friar. Come, murderous Prior.

 Much. Come, ye dog's face.

 King. Why how now, Robin ? Where's the drink you
  bring ?

 Robin. Lay hold on these!
Far be it, I should bring your Majesty
The drink these two prepared for your taste.

 King. Why, Robin Hood ? be brief and answer me.
I am amazed at thy troubled looks.

 Robin. Long will not my ill looks amaze your grace ;
I shortly look never to look again.

 Marian. Never to look ! What will it still be night ?
If thou look never, day can never be.
What ails my Robin ? Wherefore dost thou faint ?

 Robin. Because I cannot stand : yet now I can.
Thanks to my King, and thanks to Marian.

 King. Robin, be brief, and tell us what hath chanc'd.

 Robin. I must be brief, for I am sure of death,
Before a long tale can be half way told.

 Fitzwater. Of death, my son ! bright sun of all my
  joy!

Death cannot have the power of virtuous life.

Robin. Not of the virtues, but the life it can.

King. What dost thou speak of death? how shouldst
    thou die?

Robin. By poison, and the Prior's treachery.

Queen. Why, take this sovereign powder at my hands:
Take it, and live in spite of poison's power.

Doncaster. I, set him forward. Powders quoth ye? hah!
I am a fool then, if a little dust,
The shaving of a horn, a Bezar's stone,*
Or any antidote have power to stay
The execution of my heart's resolve.
Tut, tut, you labour, lovely Queen, in vain,
And on a thankless groom your toil bestow.
Now hath your foe reveng'd you of your foe:
Robin shall die if all the world said no.

Marian. How the wolf howls! Fly, like a tender kid
Into thy shepherd's bosom. Shield me love!
Canst thou not Robin? Where shall I be hid?
Oh, God! these ravens will seize upon thy dove.

Robin. They cannot hurt thee, pray thee, do not fear:
Base curs will couch, the lion being near.

Queen. How works my powder?

Robin. Very well, fair Queen.

King. Dost thou feel any ease?

Robin. I shall, I trust, anon:
Sleep falls upon mine eyes. Oh, I must sleep,
And they that love me do not waken me.

Marian. Sleep in my lap, and I will sing to thee.

John. He should not sleep.

Robin. I must, for I must die;
While I live, therefore, let me have some rest.

Fitzwater. I, let him him rest: the poison urges sleep.

---

* Or Bezoar-stone, formerly considered an antidote for poison. Sir
Thomas Brown was not prepared to contradict it: he says, that "Lapis
Lasuli hath in it a purgative faculty we know: that *Bezoar is antidotal,*
Lapis Judaicus diuretical, Coral antipileptical, we will not deny"—
Vulgar Errors, edit. 1658, p. 104. He also (p. 205) calls it the
Bezoar nut, "for being broken, it discovereth a kernel of a legumin-
ous smell and taste, bitter like a lupine, and will swell and sprout if
set in the ground." Harts-horn shavings were also considered a
preservative against poison.

When he awakes there is no hope of life.
   Doncaster. Of life! Now, by the little time I have to
     live,
He cannot live one hour for your lives.
   King. Villain! what art thou?
   Doncaster. Why, I am a knight.
   Chester. Thou wert, indeed. If it so please your
     Grace,
I will describe my knowledge of this wretch.
   King. Do, Chester.
   Chester. This Doncaster, for so the felon hight,
Was by the King, your father, made a knight,
And well in arms he did himself behave.
Many a bitter storm, the wind of rage
Blasted this realm with, in those woeful days
When the unnatural fights continued
Between your kingly father and his sons.
This cut-throat, knighted in that time of woe,
Seized on a beauteous nun, at Berkhamstead,
As we were marching toward Winchester,
After proud Lincoln was compell'd to yield.
He took this virgin straying in the field;
For all the nuns and every covent* fled
The dangers that attended on our troops:
For those sad times too oft did testify,
War's rage hath no regard to piety.
She humbly pray'd him, for the love of heaven,
To guide her to her father's, two miles thence:
He swore he would, and very well he might,
For to the camp he was a forager.
Upon the way they came into a wood,
Wherein, in brief, he stripp'd this tender maid:
Whose lust, when she in vain had long withstood,
Being by strength and torments overlaid,
He did a sacrilegious deed of rape,
And left her bath'd in her own tears and blood.
When she reviv'd, she to her father's got,
And got her father to make just complaint
Unto your mother, being then in camp.

   * The old word for *convent*: Covent-Garden, therefore, is still
properly called.

Queen. Is this the villain, Chester, that defil'd
Sir Eustace Stutville's chaste and beauteous child ?

Doncaster. I, madam, this is he,
That made a wench dance naked in a wood ;
And, for she did deny what I desired,
I scourg'd her for her pride, 'till her fair skin
With stripes was chequer'd like a vintner's grate.*
And what was this ?   A mighty matter sure!
I have a thousand more than she defil'd,
And cut the squeaking throats of some of them :
I grieve I did not hers.

Queen. Punish him, Richard.
A fairer virgin never saw the sun ;
A chaster maid was never sworn a nun.

King. How 'scap'd the villain punishment that time?

Fitzwater. I rent his spurs off, and disgraded him.

Chester. And then he rail'd upon the Queen and me.
Being committed, he his keeper slew,
And to your father fled, who pardon'd him.

Richard. God give his soul a pardon for that sin.

Salisbury. Oh, had I heard his name, or seen his face,
I had defended Robin from this chance !
Ah, villain ! shut those gloomy lights of thine.
Remember'st thou a little son of mine,
Whose nurse at Wilton first thou ravishedst,
And slew'st two maids that did attend on them ?

Doncaster. I grant I dash'd the brains out of a brat,
Thine if he were, I care not : had he been
The first born comfort of a royal king,
And should have yall'd, when Doncaster cried peace,
I would have done by him as then I did.

King. Soon shall the world be rid of such a wretch.
Let him be hang'd alive in the highway
That joineth to the Tower.†

* The *grate* of a vintner was no doubt what is often termed in old
writers the *red lattice*, *lettice*, or *chequers*, painted at the doors of
vintners, and still preserved at almost every public-house.   See
D. O. P. vol. v. note 24, to *The Miseries of inforced Marriage.*

† The 4to. reads,

——————— " in the high way
That joineth to the *power*."

Doncaster. Alive or dead, (I reck not how I die.)
You, them, and these, I desperately defy.

Ely. Repent, or never look to be absolv'd;
But die accurs'd, as thou deservest well.

Doncaster. Then give me my desert: curse one by one!

Ely. First I accurse thee; and if thou persist,
Unto damnation leave thee, wretched man.

Doncaster. What do I care for your damnation?
Am I not doomed to death? what more damnation
Can there ensue your loud and yelling cries?

Prior. Yes, devil! hear thy fellow spirit speak,
Who would repent; Oh, fain he would repent!
After this body's bitter punishment,
There is an ever-during endless woe,
A quenchless fire, an unconsuming pain
Which desperate souls and bodies must endure.

Doncaster. Can you preach this, yet set me on, Sir
          Prior,
To run into this endless, quenchless fire?

Prior. High heavens, shew mercy to my many ills!
Never had this been done, but like a fiend,
Thou tempted'st me with ceaseless devilish thoughts.
Therefore I curse with bitterness of soul
The hour wherein I saw thy baleful eyes.
My eyes I curse, for looking on those eyes!
My ears I curse, for hearkening to thy tongue!
I curse thy tongue for tempting of mine ears!
Each part I curse, that we call thine or mine;
Thine for enticing mine, mine following thine!!

Doncaster. A holy prayer.   What collect have we
          next?   [*This time Robin stirs.*

Fitzwater. My Marian wanteth words, such is her woe;
But old Fitzwater for his girl and him
Begs nothing, but world's plague for such a foe,
Which causeless harm'd a virtuous nobleman,
A pityer of his griefs, when he felt grief.
Therefore, bethink thee of thy hateful deed,
Thou faithless Prior, and thou this ruthless thief.

Prior. Will no man curse me, giving so much cause?
Then Doncaster, ourselves ourselves accurse,

And let no good betide to thee or me !
> [*All the yeomen, Friar, Much, Jenny cry.*

All. Amen, amen: accursed may he be,
For murdering Robin, flower of courtesy.
> [*Robin sits up.*

Robin. Oh, ring not such a peal for Robin's death !
Let sweet forgiveness be my passing bell.
Art thou there Marian? then fly forth my breath ;
To die within thy arms contents me well.

Prior. Keep in, keep in a little while thy soul,
Till I have pour'd my soul forth at thy feet.

Robin. I slept not, uncle ; I your grief did hear,
Let him forgive thy soul that bought it dear :
Your body's deed, I in my death forgive,
And humbly beg the king that you may live.
Stand to your clergy, uncle ;* save your life
And lead a better life than you have done.

Prior. Oh, gentle nephew ! Oh, my brother's son,
Thou dying glory of old Huntington !
Wishest thou life to such a murderous foe ?
I will not live since thou must life forego.
Oh, happy Warman ! blessed in thy end ;
Now too, too late thy truth I do commend.
Oh, nephew, nephew ! Doncaster and I
Murder'd poor Warman, for he did deny
To join with us in this black tragedy.

Robin. Alas, poor Warman ! Friar, Little John,

---

* Robin Hood advises his uncle to insist upon his plea of *privilegium clericale*, or benefit of clergy :—
> "Stand to your clergy, uncle ; save your life."

" Originally the law was held that no man should be admitted to the privilege of clergy, but such as had the *habitum et tonsuram clericalem.* But in process of time a much wider and more comprehensive criterion was established ; every one that could read (a mark of great learning in those days of ignorance and her sister superstition) being accounted a clerk, or *clericus,* and allowed the benefit of clerkship, though neither initiated in holy orders, nor trimmed with the clerical tonsure." Blackstone's Comm. iv. B 4. ch. 28. We have already seen that the king and nobles in this play called in the aid of Friar Tuck to read the inscription on the stag's collar, though the king could ascertain that it was in Saxon characters.

I told ye both where Warman's body lay,
And of his burial I'll dispose anon.

King. Is there no law, Lord Ely, to convict
This Prior, that confesses murders thus?

Ely. He is a hallow'd man, and must be tried,
And punish'd by the censure of the church.

Prior. The church therein doth err: God doth allow
No canon to preserve a murderer's life.
Richard! king Richard! in thy grandsire's day's,
A law was made, the clergy sworn thereto,
That whatsoever churchman did commit
Treason or murder, or false felony,
Should like a secular be punished.
Treason we did, for sure we did intend
King Richard's poisoning, sovereign of this land.
Murder we did in working Warman's end,
And my dear nephew's, by this fatal hand:
And theft we did, for we have robb'd the king,
The state, the nobles, commons, and his men,
Of a true peer, firm pillar, liberal lord.
Fitzwater we have robbed of a kind son,
And Marian's love-joys we have quite undone:

Doncaster. Whoop! what a coil is here with your
     confession.

Prior. I ask but judgment for my foul transgression

King. Thy own mouth hath condemn'd thee. Hence
     with him!
Hang this man dead, then see him buried;
But let the other hang alive in chains.

Doncaster. I thank you, sir.

               [*Exeunt Yeomen, Friar, Prisoners, Much.*

John. Myself will, go my lord,
And see sharp justice done upon these slaves.

Robin. Oh, go not hence, Prince John! a word or two,
Before I die, I fain would say to you.

King. Robin, we see what we are sad to see,
Death, like a champion, treading down thy life:
Yet in thy end somewhat to comfort thee,
We freely give to thy betrothed wife,
Beauteous and chaste Matilda, all those lands,

Fallen by thy folly to the Prior's hands,
And by his fault now forfeited to me.
Earl Huntington, she shall thy countess be,
And thy wight yeomen, they shall wend with me
Against the faithless enemies of Christ.

   Robin. Bring forth a bier, and cover it with green;
That on my death-bed I may here sit down.

                 [*A bier is brought in.*   *He sits.*

At Robin's burial let no black be seen,
Let no hand give for him a mourning gown;
For in his death his king hath given him life,
By this large gift, given to his maiden wife.
Chaste maid Matilda, countess of account,
Chase with thy bright eyes, all these clouds of woe
From these fair cheeks; I pray thee, sweet, do so:
Think it is bootless folly to complain
For that which never can be had again.
Queen Elinor, you once were Matild's foe;
Prince John, you long sought her unlawful love;
Let dying Robin Hood intreat you both
To change those passions: madam, turn your hate,
To princely love: prince John, convert your love
To virtuous passions, chaste and moderate.
Oh, that your gracious right hands would enfold
Matilda's right hand, prison'd in my palm,
And swear to do what Robin Hood desires!

   Queen. I swear I will: I will a mother be
To fair Matilda's life and chastity.

   John. When John solicits chaste Matilda's ears
With lawless suits, as he hath often done,
Or offers to the altars of her eyes,
Lascivious poems, stuff'd with vanities,
He craves to see but short and sour days:
His death be like to Robin's he desires;
His perjured body prove a poison'd prey,
For cowled monks, and barefoot begging friars.

   Robin. Enough, enough! Fitzwater take your child.
My dying frost, which no sun's heat can thaw,
Closes the powers of all my outward parts:

My freezing blood runs back unto my heart,
Where it assists death, which it would resist:
Only my love a little hinders death,
For he beholds her eyes, and cannot smite:
Then go not yet Matilda, stay awhile.
Friar make speed, and list my latest will.

   Matilda. Oh, let me look for ever in thy eyes,
And lay my warm breath to thy bloodless lips,
If my sight can restrain death's tyrannies,
Or keep life's breath within thy bosom lock'd.

   Robin. Away, away!
Forbear my love; all this is but delay.

   Fitzwater. Come, maiden daughter, from my maiden
      son,
And give him leave to do what must be done.

   Robin. First, I bequeath my soul to all souls' Saver,
And will my body to be buried
At Wakefield, underneath the Abbey wall;
And in this order make my funeral.
When I am dead stretch me upon this bier:
My beads and primer shall my pillow be;
On this side be my bow, my good shafts here;
Upon my breast the cross, and underneath
My trusty sword, thus fasten'd in the sheath.
Let Warman's body at my feet be laid,
Poor Warman, that in my defence did die.
For holy dirges sing me woodmen's songs,
As ye to Wakefield walk with voices shrill.
This for myself.   My goods and plate I give
Among my yeomen: them I do bestow.
Upon my sovereign, Richard.   This is all.
My liege, farewell! my love, farewell, farewell!
Farewell fair queen, prince John, and noble lords!
Father Fitzwater, heartily adieu!
Adieu, my yeomen tall.   Matilda, close mine eyes.
Friar, farewell! farewell to all!

   Matilda. Oh, must my hands with envious death
      conspire
To shut the morning gates of my life's light!

Fitzwater. It is a duty, and thy love's desire :
I'll help thee, girl, to close up Robin's sight.*

King. Laments are bootless, tears cannot restore
Lost life, Matilda ; therefore weep no more :
And since our mirth is turned into moan,
Our merry sport to tragic funeral,
We will prepare our power for Austria,
After Earl Robert's timeless burial.
Fall to your wood-songs, therefore, yeomen bold,
And deck his hearse with flowers that lov'd you dear :
Dispose his goods as he hath them dispos'd.
Fitzwater and Matilda, bide you here.
See you the body unto Wakefield borne :
A little we will bear ye company,
But all of us at London 'point to meet :
Thither, Fitzwater, bring Earl Robin's men ;
And, Friar, see you come along with them.

Friar. Ah, my liege lord, the Friar faints,
And hath no words to make complaints ;
But since he must forsake this place,
He will await, and thanks your grace.

SONG.

Weep, weep, ye woodmen wail,
Your hands with sorrow wring ;
Your master Robin Hood lies dead,
Therefore sigh as you sing.

Here lie his primer and his beads,
His bent bow and his arrows keen,
His good sword and his holy cross :
Now cast on flowers fresh and green ;

And as they full shed tears and say,
Wella, wella-day, wella, wella-day :
Thus cast ye flowers and sing,
And on to Wakefield take your way.   [*Exeunt.*

* This account of the death of Robin Hood varies from all the
popular narratives and ballads. The MS. Sloan, 715, nu. 7, f. 157,
agrees with the ballad in Ritson (ii. 183), that he was treacherously
bled to death by the Prioress of Kirksley.

D

Friar. Here doth the Friar leave with grievance;
Robin is dead that graced his entrance,
And being dead, he craves his audience
With this short play they would have patience.*
                    Enter CHESTER.
Chester. Nay, Friar, at request of thy kind friend,
Let not thy play too soon be at an end.
Though Robin Hood be dead, his yeomen gone,
And that thou think'st there now remains not one,
To act another scene or two for thee,
Yet know full well, to please this company,
We mean to end Matilda's tragedy.
    Friar. Off then, I wish you, with your Kendal green;
' Let not sad grief in fresh array be seen.
Matilda's story is replete with tears,
Wrongs, desolations, ruins, deadly fears.
In, and attire ye.   Though I tired be,
Yet will I tell my mistress' tragedy.
Apollo's masterdom† I invocate,
To whom henceforth my deeds I dedicate;
That of his godhead, 'bove all gods divine,
With his rich spirit he would lighten mine :
That I may sing true lays of trothless deeds,
Which to conceive my heart through sorrow bleeds.
Cheer thee, sad soul, and in a lofty line
Thunder out wrong, compast in cloudy tears:
                    [*Enter in black.*‡

    * The first act has already occupied too much space, but it was
difficult to divide it : in fact, as Friar Tuck says, it is a " short play,"
complete in itself.   What follows is an Induction to the rest of the
story, the Friar continuing on the stage after the others have gone out.
    † The 4to reads thus,—
            " Apollo's *master doone* I invocate,"
but probably we ought to read—
            " Apollo's *masterdom* I invocate ;"
and the text has been altered accordingly : *masterdom* means *power,
rule* ; to invocate Apollo's masterdom, is therefore to invocate
Apollo's power to assist the Friar in his undertaking.
    ‡ " Enter in black" is the whole of the stage direction, and those
who enter are afterwards designated by the letters *Cho.* Perhaps
the principal performers arrive attired in black, and are mentioned as
Chorus, one speaking for the rest.   *Cho.* may, however, be a misprint
for *Chester,* who was sent in to " attire him."

Shew to the eyes, fill the beholders ears,
With all the lively acts of lustful rage,
Restrain'd by modest tears, and chastity's intreats:
And let king John, that ill-part personage,
By suits, devices, practices and threats,
And when he sees all serveth to no end,
Of chaste Matilda let him make an end.

Cho. We are all fitted, Friar: shall we begin?

Friar. Well art thou suited: would my order would
Permit me habit equal to my heart!

Cho. If you remember, John did take an oath
Never again to seek Matilda's love.

Friar. O what is he, that's sworn affection's slave,
That will not violate all laws, all oaths?
And being mighty, what will he omit
To compass his intents, though ne'er so ill?—
You must suppose king Richard now is dead,
And John (resistless) is fair England's lord;
Who striving to forget Matilda's love,
Takes to his wife the beauteous Isabel,
Betroth'd to Hugh de Brun, Earl of North March:*
And picking quarrels under show of kin,
Wholly divorces his first queen away.
But yet Matilda still, still troubles him,
And being in the court, so oft he courts her,
That by her noble father, old Fitzwater,
She is remov'd from his lust-tempting eye.
But tides restrain'd o'erswell their bounds with rage:
Her absence adds more fuel to his fire.
In sleep he sees her, and his waking thoughts
Study by day to compass his desire.

Cho. Friar, since now you speak of visions,
It was received by tradition
From those that were right near unto king John,

* This name ought to be Hugh *le* Brun, and not Hugh *de* Brun:
"John married Isabel the daughter and heiress of the Earl of Angou-
lesme, who was before affianced to *Hugh le Brun*, Earl of March, (a
peer of great estate and excellence in France) by the consent of king
Richard in whose custody she then was."
                              Samuel Daniel's History of England.

Of three strange visions that to him appear'd;
And, as I guess, I told you what they were.
    Friar. With them I will begin. Draw but that veil,
And there king John sits sleeping in his chair.
    [*Draw the curtain: the king sits sleeping, his sword by
      his side. Enter Austria, before whom cometh Ambi-
      tion, and bringing him before the chair, King John,
      in sleep, maketh signs to avoid, and holdeth his own
      crown fast with both his hands.*
    Friar. Ambition, that had ever waited on king John,
Now brings him Austria, easy to be ta'en,
Being wholly tam'd by Richard's warlike hand,
And bids him add that dukedom to his crown:
But he puts by Ambition, and contemns
.All other kingdoms but the English crown,
Which he holds fast as if he would not lose.
    [*Enter Constance, leading Young Arthur: both offer
      to take the crown; but with his foot he overturneth
      them: to them cometh Insurrection, led by the F. K.
      and L,* menacing him, and leads the child again to
      the chair; but he only layeth hand on his sword,
      and with his foot overthroweth the child, whom they
      take up as dead; and Insurrection flying they mourn-
      fully bear in the body.*
    Friar. The lady and the child that did ascend,
Striving in vain to take the crown from John,
Were Constance and her son the Duke of Britaine,
Heir to the elder brother of the king:
Yet he sleeps on, and with a little spurn
The mother and the prince doth overturn.
Again, when Insurrection them assists,
Stirr'd by the French king and the wronged earl,
Whose troth-plight wife king John had ta'en to wife,
He only claps his hand upon his sword,
Mocketh their threatenings, and in their attempts
The harmless prince receives recureless death,
Whom they, too late, with bootless tears lament.

    * "Led by F. K. and L." means, as afterwards appears, the
French King, and *Lord* Hugh de Brun, Earl of North March.

[*Enter Queen with two Children borne after her : she ascends, and seeing no motion, she fetcheth her Children one by one; but seeing yet no motion, she descendeth wringing her hands, and departeth. Enter Matilda in a mourning veil, reading on a book, at whose coming he starteth, and sitteth upright : as she passeth by he smiles, and folds his arms as if he did embrace her : being gone, he starts suddenly and speaks.*

King. Matilda ! stay Matilda, do but speak !
Who's there ? Entreat Maltilda to come back.

Enter BONVILLE.*

Bonville. Who would you have, my lord ?
King. Why, my Lord Bonville, I would have Matilda,
That but even now pass'd by toward the door.
Bonville. I saw her not, my lord.
King. Hadst thou a lover's eye,
A gnat, a mote, a shadow thou would'st spy.
Come, follow me ; she cannot be so far,
But I shall overtake her : come, away !   [*Exeunt.*
Friar. The last appearance shadow'd the fair Queen,
And her two children, at whose sight King John
Shewed neither sign nor shew of passion :.
But when the sun came masked in a cloud,
And veiled beauty, join'd with chastity,
Appeared in Matilda's lovely shape,
He starts, he clasps, he wakes, he calls, he seeks
The shadow of that substance he affects.
To her he sues, but she his suit rejects ;
To him she sues, but he her suit neglects :
He sues to be her love; she doth despise :
She sues to live a maid, which he denies.
What follows of this wilfull will and shall,
This no and nay, this quenchless, bootless fire,
This cold affection, and this hot desire,
The act itself shall tell ; and the poor Friar
Your partial favours humbly doth require.   [*Exit.*

* The entrance of Bonville is omitted in the 4to. 1601.

ACT II. SCENE I.

Sound trumpets. Enter KING, BONVILLE, SALISBURY,
LORDS.*

King. Now I perceive this only was a dream.
Divine Matilda's angel did appear,
Deck'd like a vestal ready for heaven's quire,
And to this earthly trunk will not come near.
Well, let her go: I must, 'ifaith, I must,
And so I will.   King's thoughts should be divine;
So are Matilda's, so henceforth shall mine.
      Old Aubery. So doing, peace shall wait upon your
            crown,
And blessing upon blessing shall befall.
      King. It's true my lord: I know full well there shall.
      Salisbury. Your people will wax proud of such a king,
That of himself is king, lord of his thoughts;
Which by assertion of philosophers,
Is held to be the greatest empery.
      King. And they said wisely, noble Aubery.
      Salisbury. Then will Fitzwater, with his gallant troops,
Again keep triumphs in the English court;
Then will Matilda——
      King. Matilda! what of her?
      Salisbury. Like a bright star adorn the lovely train
Of beauteous ladies which attend the Queen,
Whose only beauty equalleth them all.
      King. Like an old fool, whose dim eyes, wanting sight,
Compar'st the sun to common candle light.
      Salisbury. Pardon, my liege, I do confess, her fair†

---

      * These *Lords*, as we afterwards find, are old Aubery de Vere,
Hubert, and Mowbray.
      † Lodge was in the habit of using the adjective for the substantive,
especially *fair* for *fairness:* one example is enough.
            " Some, well I wot, and of that some full many,
            Wisht or my *faire* or their desire were lesse."
                                    Scilla's Metamorphosis, 1589.
      See also note 16 to *The Wounds of Civil War*, D. O. P. vol. viii.
      Shakespeare may be cited in many places besides the following.

Exceeds all these as far as day doth night.

   King. Grossly alluded : night by moon, by stars
By wandering fires, exhaled meteors,
By artificial lights, by eyes of beasts,
And little glow-worms glimpsing in the dark,
Hath somewhere brightness, lightness ; and sometime,
Under each horizon in all parts clear:
But they at no time, no where, can be said
To be less dark than dungeon darkness is,
Pitch-colour'd, ebon-fac'd, blacker than black,
While her fair eyes give beauty to bright day.

   Salisbury. To hear the queen thus prais'd works my
      content.

   King. The queen!
Oh, had I such a thought I would repent.   [*to himself.*

   Salisbury. Further my lord——

   King. What, shall we further wade?
I fear I shall be tired with this jade.

   Salisbury. The common-wealth will flourish and in-
      crease.

   King. Good Salisbury,* of those things now hold your
      peace,
And take the pains to fetch in Isabel.
I have strange tidings sent me out of France,
Which she will take, I know, in as good part,
As I accept her praise.   Fetch her, I say.
                        [Exit Salisbury.
What, is the old fool gone? now go thy way.
What think'st thou of him, Hubert? tell me, man.

   Hubert. As of a good old gentleman, my lord,
That speaks but what he thinks, and thinks you think
As he doth ; and, I warrant you,

       —— " My decayed *fair*
   A sunny look of his would soon repair."
               Comedy of Errors, Act ii. sc. 1.
See Steevens's note on the above passage.

  * The King calls him in the old copy "*good Oxford*," but Oxford
is not present, and from what follows we see that the command was
given to Salisbury. The same mistake is again made by Hubert
in this scene. Salisbury must be pronounced *Sal'sb'ry.*

Will not conceal those praises from the Queen,
Which, as he deems, you utter'd in her praise.

   King. I would have them believe it so, indeed;
But I protest 'tis no part of my creed.

   Hubert. I'faith, your grace did Salisbury's years great
       wrong,
To curtail his good work, that seem'd so long:
He, peradventure, would have brought in more,
After his preface, to rich plenty's store.
Perchance he would have shew'd dame vanity,
That in your court is suffered hourly;
And bade you punish ruffians with long hair,
New fashions, and such toys. A special care
Has that good man: he turns the statute book;
About his hall and chambers, if you look,
The moral virtues in fair effigy
Are lively painted: moral philosophy
Has not a sentence, be it great or small,
But it is painted on his honour's wall.

       Enter QUEEN *and* SALISBURY.

   King. Peace, peace! he comes: now let's be silent all.

   Salisbury. I tell you, I was proud of his good words.

   Queen. God hold them, Salisbury; for it's often seen,
A reconciled foe small good affords.

   Salisbury. Oh, forbear! trust me,
I gage my honour he doth hold you dear.

   King. How cheer you, Isabel? The Earl your spouse
Hath sent defiance to the King your husband,
And, like a tried tall soldier, fled his holds
In Marchland; where he knows, despight of him
And all the men that he therein can raise,
King John could have sent dogs enow to tear
Their ill arm'd bodies piece-meal, ere his bands
Should with base blood have stain'd their noble hands.
And whither is this worshipful good earl
(This first love, old love, new love, if you will)
Gone, thinks your ladyship? forsooth, good man,
To Normandy; and there he stirs up coals,
And urgeth strong aid for confederates,
Who, as he says, are treacherously disposed.

Queen. If he do so the greater is his sin.
Poor man, I have no interest in him.
  King. But he hath had in you, as it should seem,
Else would he not make sonnets of your brow,
Your eye, your lip, your hand, your thigh.
A plague upon him ! how came he so nigh?
Nay, now you have the curst quean's counterfeit:
Through rage you shake, because you cannot rave.
But answer me : why should the Bedlam slave
Entitle a whole poem to your kiss,
Calling it cherry, ruby, this and this?
I tell you, I am jealous of your love,
Which makes me break into this passion.
Here's the kind noble Aubery de Vere,
Knows what I speak is true.
My lord, my lord ! I do appeal to you,
Are these things to be borne ?
  Salisbury. No, by the rood :
These love rhimes are the tokens of small good.
  Hubert. Why, my good lord, was never poetry
Offer'd unto a lady's patronage?
  Salisbury. Yes, but not taken.
  Hubert. Yes, and taken too.
Though muddy slaves, whose balladizing rhimes
With words unpolished shew their brutish thoughts,
Naming their maukins in each lustful line,
Let no celestial beauty look awry,
When well-writ poems, couching her rich praise,
Are offer'd to her unstain'd virtuous eye :
For poetry's high sprighted sons will raise
True beauty to all wish'd eternity.
Therefore, my lord, your age is much to blame
To think a taken poem lady's shame.
  Salisbury. You see the King, that's better read than you,
And far more wrong'd than I, takes it not well.
  King. Yes, but I do : I think not Isabel
The worse for any writing of Lord Brun's.*

* In the old copy it stands thus :
    " Yes, but I do : I think not Isabel, Lord,
      The worse for any writing of Brun's."
The word " Lord," by some accident has been transferr'd from the
last to the first of the two lines, to the injury of the sense and metre.

Salisbury. Will you ha' the truth my lord? I think so
    too;
And though I be an old man, by my sword,
My arm shall justify my constant word.
    Queen. After a long storm in a troublous sea,
The pilot is no gladder of a calm,
Than Isabel to see the vexed looks
Of her lov'd lord chang'd into sweet aspects.
    King. I will not tell thee what a world of foes
For thy love (dear love) rise against my life.
Matilda's love; few swords will fight for thee.

                                  [to himself.

I will not number up the many woes
That shall be multiplied: strife upon strife
Will follow; but to shun ensuing ills,
I'll take such pledges as shall please me ask
Of each proud baron dwelling in the realm.
Bruce, kinsman and the deputy to March,
Hath a high-minded lady to his wife,
An able son for arms, and a less boy
That is the comfort of his father's life.
Madam, I know you love the lady well,
And of her wealth you may be bold to build,
By sending you four hundred white milch kine,
And ten like-colour'd bulls to serve that herd;
So fair, that every cow did Iö seem,
And every bull Europa's ravisher.
To friend myself with such a subject's truth,
Thus I command: you and Earl Salisbury
Shall, with what speed conveniently ye may,
Hie ye to Guildford: there the lady lies,
And her sons too, as I am told by spies.
All that she hath, I know, she calleth your's;
All that she hath, I gladly would call mine,
If she abuse ye: if she use ye well,
For ever be what she retains her own.
Only go by, as queens in progress do,
And send me word how she receiveth you.
    Queen. Well, I avouch she will, before I go:
Far be it, John should prove Lord Bruce's foe.

Come, noble Salisbury I long to be at Guildford.

Salisbury. In such a business, madam, so do I.

[*Exeunt.*

King. Go on, good stales:* now Guildford is mine
    own!
Hubert, I charge you take an hundred horse,
And follow unto Guildford castle gates.
The Queen pretend you come to tend upon,
Sent carefully from us: when you are in,
Boldly demand the lady for her sons,
For pledges of her husband's faith and her's:
Whom when ye have upon the castle seize,
And keep it to our use until we come.
Meanwhile let me alone with Hugh, your son,
To work a wonder, if no prodigy;
But, whatsoe'er, it shall attempted be.

Hubert. Even that which to your majesty
May seem contentful, therefore I agree.

King. Go then to Guildford, and a victor be.

[*Exit Hubert.*

Mowbray, our mask: are you and Chester ready?

Mowbray. We will before your grace, I warrant you.

King. How think'st of it, Mowbray?

Mowbray. As on a mask: but for our torch bearers,
Hell cannot rake so mad a crew as I.

King. Faith, who is chief?

Mowbray. Will Brand, my lord;
But then your Grace must curb his cruelty:
The rein once got, he's apt for villany.

King. I know the villain is both rough and grim;
But as a tie-dog I will muzzle him.
I'll bring him up to fawn upon my friends,
And worry dead my foes. But to our mask.
I mean this night to revel at the feast,
Where fair Matilda graceth every guest;
And if my hidden courtesy she grace,

---

* See the notes of Dr. Jóhnson, Steevens and other commentators
on the words in the *Comedy of Errors*, Act II. sc. 1. " Poor I am
but his *stale*."

Old Baynard's Castle, good Fitzwater's place,
John will make rich, with royal England's wealth :
But if she do not, not those scatter'd bands,
Dropping from Austria and the Holy Land,
That boast so much of glorious victories,
Shall stop the inundations of those woes,
That like a deluge I will bring on them.
I know the crew is there, banish all fears :
If wronged they shall be our's, if welcome theirs.

[Exeunt.

SCENE II.

Enter Fitzwater, *and his* Son : Old Bruce *and*
Young Bruce, *and call forth* Matilda.*

Fitzwater. Why how now, votary ! still at your book ?
Ever in mourning weeds?   For shame, for shame !
With better entertainment cheer our friends.
Now, by the blest cross, you are much to blame
To cross our mirth thus ; you are much to blame, I say.
Good lord ! hath never woe enough of welladay ?
Indeed, indeed,
Some sorrow fits, but this is more than need.
    Matilda. Good father, pardon me :
You saw I sate the supper and the banquet;
You know I cannot dance ; discourse I shun,
By reason that my wit, but small before,
Comes far behind the ripe wits of our age.
    Young Bruce. You'll be too ripe for marriage,
If you delay by day and day, thus long.
There is the noble Wigmore, Lord of the March
That lies on Wye, Lug, and the Severn streams :
His son is like the sun's sire's Ganymede,
And for your love hath sent a lord to plead.

---

* The stage directions are often given very confusedly, and take
by themselves unintelligibly, in the old copy, of which this instance
may serve as a specimen: it stands thus in the 4to. " Enter Fits-
water and his Son Bruce, and call forth his daughter."

His absence I did purpose to excuse,
> *Enter* LEICESTER.

But Leicester is the man for him that sues.

   Fitzwater. My cousin Bruce hath been your broker,
      Leicester;
At least hath broke the matter to my girl.

   Leicester. Oh, for a barber at the time of need,
Or one of these that dresses periwigs,
To deck my grey head with a youthful hair!
But I must to't. Matilda thus it is:
Say can ye love me? I am Wigmore's son.

   Matilda. My cousin said he look'd like Ganymede;
But you, but you—

   Leicester. But I, but I, you say,
Am rather like old Chremes in a play;*
But that's a nice objection: I am he,
But by attorneyship made deputy.

   Matilda. He's never like to speed well, all his life,
That by attorney sues to win a wife:
But grant you are whom you seem nothing like,
Young Wigmore, the heir to this noble lord,
He for his son hath sent us ne'er a word.

   Old Bruce. If you grant love when his son doth woo,
Then in your jointure he'll send, say, and do.

   Young. Bruce. And for a doer cousin, take my word:
Look for a good egg, he was a good bird;
Cock o' the game, i'faith, never fear.

   Matilda. I, but I fear the match will fall out ill,
Because he says his son is named Will.

   Fitzwater. And why, good daughter? hath some
      palmister,
Some augur, or some dreaming calculator,
(For such, I know, you often hearken to)
Been prating 'gainst the name? go to, go to;
Do not believe them. Leicester fall to woo.

---

  * Alluding most likely to the *Andria* of Terence, which had been translated twice before this play was acted; the first time anonymously printed (as it is supposed) by J. Rastell; secondly by Maurice Kiffin, in 1588.

Matilda. I must believe my father; and 'tis you,
That if I ought misdid, reprov'd me still,
And chiding said, " you're wedded to your will."

    Fitzwater. God, for thy mercy! have ye catch'd me
       there?
Wigmore is William, woman. Leicester, speak:
Thou art the simplest wooer in the world.

    Leicester. You have put me out, and she hath took
       me down;
You with your talk, she with her ready tongue.
You told me I should find her mild and still,
And scarce a word came from her in an hour:
Then did I think I should have all the talk,
Unhinder'd by your willingness to help,
Unanswer'd 'till I had no more to say;
And then—

    Young Bruce. What then?
She with a courtly court'sy saying nay.

    Matilda. Your friend's attorney might have gone
      his way
With as great credit as did that orator,
Which handling an oration some three hours,
Ill for the matter, worse than bad for phrase,
Having said *diri*, look'd, and found not one,
To praise or dispraise his oration;
For wearied with his talk they all were gone.

    Fitzwater. Now, by my troth, if any troth I have,
I am as merry at Matilda's mirth,
As I was glad to see her first day's birth.
For 'till this hour, so help me Holidom,*
Since the too timely death of Huntington,
Not a blithe word had passage through her lips.

    Leicester. See what a pleasing humour wooers bring.
    Young Bruce. Oh, but ye leave too soon.
    Leicester. Yet she avers,

---

* *Holidom* or *halidom* according to Minshieu (Dicty. 1617) is " an old word used by old country women, by manner of swearing by my *halidome*; of the Saxon word *haligdome*, *ex halig, sanctum*, and *dome, dominium aut judicium.*" Shakespeare puts it into the mouth of the host in the *Two Gentlemen of Verona.* Act iv. scene 2.

I stand too long: shall I chuse your's or her's?
   Matilda. Either forbear, I pray ye, for a while.
Enter RICHMOND.*

Welcome Lord Richmond.
   Richmond. What doth Matilda smile,
That still like silence solitary sat?
Then, off with widow's weeds, and teach your feet
(That have forgot for want of exercise,
And by the means your sorrow had no mean)
To tread a measure, for a gallant crew
Of courtly maskers landed at the stairs ;
Before whom, unintreated, I am come,
And have prevented, I believe, their page,
Who with his torch is enter'd.
   Fitzwater. Richmond, thanks,
If you have aught to say about the maskers.
Beseech the gentlemen to enter in,
For they are welcome guests to old Fitzwater.
[*Exit Messenger.*

Son, son, I pray you fetch the ladies in :
We have been talking here about a match,
And left our noble friends in discontent.
   Richmond. Nay, by my faith, we had much merri-
      ment,
Yet thought it long you neither came nor sent.
[*Matilda faints, and sits down.*

   Fitzwater. How now, Matilda? pray thee, cheer thee,
      girl.
   Matilda. I thought it was a lightening before death,
Too sudden to be certain. Good pleasure, stay.
Enter LADIES.

Wilt thou not, wanton? churl, then go thy way.
   Richmond. What, chang'd so soon? so soon fallen
      to your dumps?
Cheerly! the mask comes in. [*Enter the Mask.*] Oh
      God, this veil
And look fit not this sport.

---

  * The entrance of Richmond clearly takes place here, but in the
4to. he is said to come in with Leicester.

Matilda. I'll leave it.

Leicester. Nay,

For your love William's sake, fair maiden stay!

> [*Dance : maskers take each a lady, John,
> Matilda, but refusing, father.**

Fitzwater. This is no courtship, daughter; be not
nice,

You both abuse him and disparage us.

His fellows had the ladies they did chuse,

And well you know here's no more maids than Maud :†

Yourself are all our store.   I pray you, rise,

Or, by my faith, I say you do us wrong.

Matilda. I will do what you will.   Lead, lead your
dance.

King. You know me by my speech.

Matilda. I, my liege, I.   Oh, that temptation's tongue
Had no where to be plac'd but in your head !

King. Well, say I have her tongue, had I not need,
When you have both her eyes, nay, all her shape,
Able to tempt even Jove himself to rape?

Matilda. Good my lord, leave, or I will leave the
place.

> [*Dance again ; and in the first course Matilda flings
> from him : John follows.*

Fitzwater. Dance out your galliard : God's dear
holybread !

Y' are too forgetful.   Dance, or by my troth,
You'll move my patience more than I will speak.

> [*She unwilling, John roughly pulls her.*

Nay soft, unmanner'd sir ; you are too rough :

Her joints are weak, your arms are strong and tough.

If ye come here for sport, you welcome be,

If not, better your room than such bad company.

> [*John threatens him by signs.*

Dost threaten me? then will I see thy face.

* Meaning that her father Fitzwater speaks, and thus reproves
her for her reluctance.   The whole account of the mask is confused
in the old copy, and it is not easy to make it much more intelligible
in the reprint.

† This is a proverb.   In Camden's Remains, by Philpot, 1636,
p. 308, it is given ; "There's no more maids than Maukin."

King. And so thou shalt. Look on me, rebel lord!
Thou that wert late a factious ring-leader,
And in the open-field gav'st me fierce fight:
Art thou again gathering another head,
That with such rudeness thou dost entertain
The gentle coming of thy sovereign?

    Fitzwater. My dread lord, hear me, and forgive this
       fault.
What I have erst done long since you forgave:
If I did lead the barons in the field,
The barons chose me, when they could not chuse
But make some leader, you were so misled.
When better thoughts enter'd your royal breast,
We then obey'd you as our sovereign head.

    King. You did even what you list, and so do still:
I am the king, but you must have your will.
The plain truth is, we are not come in sport,
Though for our coming this was our best cloke;
For if we never come 'till you do send,
·We must not be your guest while banquets last.
Contentious brawls you hourly send to us;
But we may send and send, and you return,
This lord is sick, that pained with the gout,
He rid from home. You think I find not out
Your close confederacies: yes, I do, no doubt.

    Leicester. If there be here a close confederate,
God's vengeance light upon him with my hate.

    King. No, you are open, Leicester, that I know.

    Chester. I, by the lord, my lord, your open foe.

    Leicester. By thy lord's lord, and mine, proud Ralph
       of Chester,
Thou durst not say so, wert thou from the king.

    Mowbray. Yes, but he dares and shall.

    Richmond. Mowbray, if you stand by,
He dares perchance; else will the dastard fly.

    Chester. My own sword shall maintain my tongue's
       true speech;
For it is not frequented to such lies,
As wrangling Leicester, and proud Richmond use:
It cannot set out, like a thundering drum,

Or roaring cannon, stuff'd with nought but brags,
The multitudes of seas dyed red with blood,*
And famous cities into cinders turn'd,
By their two armed arms.

   King. I, Chester;
And then they shew us rags, torn off, belike,
From poor decayed ladies' petticoats;
For neither bill, nor feather'd shot, nor pike
Make half, nor any, of those rents they have.
These, patch'd together, fasten'd unto staves,
They will not stick to swear have been advanc'd
Against the Sophi, Soldan, and the Turk.

   Leicester. Do not maintain proud Chester, my life's
     liege:
Your words I must put up; his if I bear——

   King.† Yes, you shall bear them, bear, and yet not
     bite :
We have you muzzled now. Remember once
You brav'd us with your bombard boasting words.
Come briefly, Leicester, Richmond, both Fitzwaters,
     Bruce,
Deliver up your swords immediately ;
And either yield your bodies to our hands,
Or give such pledges, as we shall accept,
Unto our steward, Winchester, with speed.

   Leicester. I will not leave my arms, nor break my
     word
Except I be provok'd : your liege-man I am sworn ;
That oath is pledge enough. If you mislike——

   King. Thou hear'st me say, I do.

   Leicester. And I reply,
That pledge refus'd, I have no more for you.

   Richmond. And Richmond says as noble Leicester
     saith.

* This line will remind the reader of Shakespeare's " multitudin-
ous seas incarnardine," in *Macbeth*, Act ii. scene 2.

† This answer unquestionably belongs to the king, and is not, as the
4to. gives it, a part of what Leicester says. It opens with an allusion
to the crest of Leicester, similar to that noticed in the *Downfall of
Huntington*.

Already have we plighted fame and faith :
Which, being scorn'd, returns to us again,
And by the king's own mouth we are discharged.
    King. Fitzwater, what say you?
    Fitzwater. What pledge desires my liege?
    King. I ask your stubborn daughter.
    Young Bruce. That were a gage
To be engaged.
    Fitzwater. Peace, thou headstrong boy.
Pardon me, sovereign ; all my power is your's ;
My goods you may command, my life you may :
My children too, I know, with both their lives,
Will readily adventure death's worst wrongs,
To do such service as true subjects should ;
But honourable fame, true chastity——
    King. Make no exceptions : yield her up to me,
Or look for ever for my enmity.
    Fitzwater. Nay then, Fitzwater tells your majesty,
You do him wrong ; and well will let you wit,
He will defend his honour to the death.
    King. And, Bruce, you are no otherwise disposed :
You will not give your sons to me for pledge.
    Bruce. I have but one, being my lesser boy,
Who is at Guildford : for my other son——
    King. He braves me with the rest.
Well, it is night, and there's no sun to swear by,
But by God's son ; and by him I here protest
A miserable storm this night to raise
That shall not cease, while England giveth rest
To such vile traitors. Bruce, I'll begin with you ;
I will, i'faith, as true as God is true.
                  [*Exit king, cum suis.*
    Leicester. Then shall a storm be rais'd against a
        storm,
And tempest be with tempest beaten back.
    Fitzwater. But this firm island, like the sea will toss.
And many goodly buildings go to wrack ;
Many a widow weep her dying son,
And many a mother to her weeping babes
Cry out uncomfortably, "children, peace,

Your crying unto me is all in vain,
Dead is my husband, your poor father slain !"
  Young Bruce. We cannot help it, uncle.
  Richmond. No, you see
Entreats and humble suits have now no power,
But lust and wrath the kingdom do devour.
  Bruce. Me he did menace first, and much I fear
He will to Guildford, and besiege my wife.
  Fitzwater. Oh, hie to save her! Richmond, ride with him.
  Richmond. Let us away, Bruce, lest we come too late,
And with us take some score of men well arm'd.
                        [Exeunt Richmond and Bruce.
  Fitzwater. Do: Leicester and myself will keep the
      city,
Till we are furnish'd with an able army.
Your nephew, Bruce, shall take an hundred armed men,
And post to Hertford castle with your sister.
Sith wrong will wake us, we will keep such watch,
As, for his life, he shall not hurt us bring.
                              [Exeunt omnes.

ACT III.   SCENE I.

Enter QUEEN, BRUCE's LADY, HUBERT, SALISBURY.
  Queen. Be comforted, good madam, do not fear,
But give your son as pledge unto the king:
Yourself at court may keep him company.
  Lady Bruce. I am betray'd! alas, I am betray'd !
And little thought your highness had been bent
So much against me for my many loves,
As to prepare an entrance for my foe.
  Queen. As I shall live in heaven, I did not know
Of Hubert's coming.   But lament not this :
Your son you say is gone ; what fear you then ?
  Lady Bruce. Oh, madam, murder, mischief, wrongs
    of men
I fear, I fear—what is't I do not fear,
Sith hope is so far off, despair so near ?
  Salisbury. Answer me, good Hubert, I pray thee,
    Hubert, do ;

What think you of this matter? may I on your word
Persuade the woman that all things are well?
   Hubert. You may persuade her if you can my_ lord;
For I protest I know no other thing,
But that the king would have him for a pledge
Of the Lord Bruce's faith.
   Salisbury. And reason too.
Now by my honour Hubert I protest
It is good reason : Bruce, I tell you plain,
Is no sound cloke to keep John from the rain.
I will go to her.
   Hubert. Do, good simple earl.
If not by threats, nor my entreats she yield,
Thy brain is barren of invention,
Dried up with care ; and never will she yield
Her son to thee, that having power want'st wit.
   Lady Bruce. I overhear thee, Hubert.
   Salisbury. So do I, dame Bruce ;
But stir no coals: the man is well belov'd,
And merits more than so.
   Lady Bruce. But I will answer.
Hubert, thou fatal keeper of poor babes,
That are appointed hostages for John,*
Had I a son here, as I have not one,
(For yesterday I sent him into Wales)
Think'st thou I would be so degenerate,
So far from kind, to give him unto thee?
I would not I protest : thou know'st my mind.
   Salisbury. Lady you fear more than you need to do :
Indeed you do ; in very deed you do.
Hubert is wrong'd about the thing you mean,
About young Arthur: Oh, I thought 'twas so :
Indeed the honest, good, kind, gentleman
Did all he might for safeguard of the child.
   Queen. Believe me, madam Bruce, the man is wrong'd.
   Lady Bruce. But he wrongs me to keep my castle
      thus,
Disarming my true servants, arming his.
Now, more of outrage ! comes what shall I do ?

* This and other passages refer, probably, to the old play of *King
John*, printed in 1591.

Enter the KING, MOWBRAY, WINCHESTER, CHESTER.

King. Oh, this is well! Hubert, where's Bruce's son?

Lady Bruce. Where thou shalt never see him, John.

King. Lady, we will have talk with you anon.
Where is he Hubert?

Hubert. Hid, or fled, my lord:
We can by no means get her to confess.

  Salisbury. Welcome to Guildford, Salisbury's liefest
       lord.*

  King. You scarce give welcome ere I bid you go;
For you, my lord, the queen, and Winchester,
Shall march to Hertford. Sweet Isabel,
And if thou love me, play the amazon.
Matilda that hath long bewitch'd mine eye
Is, as I hear by spials, now in Hertford castle:
Besiege her there; for now her haughty father
Ruffians it up and down, and all the brood
Of viperous traitors whet their poison'd teeth,
That they may feed on us that foster them.
Go forward, and go with you victory;
Which to assure, my powers shall follow you.

  Salisbury. Did I not tell you this? then trust me next.
Nay, he is chang'd, and cares no more for her,
Than I do, madam.

  King. Begone, I say begone!
Your speed rich victory attendeth on:
But your delay
May give your foes the happy glorious day.

  Queen. One boon, my liege, and part.

  King. Be brief.

  Queen. Shew that poor lady pity, I beseech. [*Exeunt.*

  King. I will indeed. Come, lady, let us in.
You have a son; go in and bring him me,
And for the queen's sake I will favour ye.

  Lady Bruce. I have no son. Come, come; come in
       and search,
And if you find him wretched may I be.   [*Exit.*

  King. Chester and Hubert, see you keep good watch.
Nor far off do I hear a warlike sound:

  * In this line, in the old copy, Salisbury is made to call himself
Oxford.

Bruce on my life! look to't while I go in
To seek this boy, for needs we must have him.
Come with us, Mowbray.

SCENE II.

Enter BRUCE, RICHMOND, SOLDIERS.

Richmond. The castle gates are shut. What ho,
  what ho.!
You that are servants to the lady Bruce,
Arise, make entrance for your lord and friends.
  Enter, or above, HUBERT, CHESTER.*
Hubert. We will make issue ere ye enter here.
Who have we there? Richmond and Bruce, is't you?
What, up so soon? are ye so early here?
In you, i'faith, the proverb's verified,
Y'are early up, and yet are ne'er the near.
  Richmond. The worse our fortune. Bruce, let us go
  hence ;
We have no power to fight, nor make defence.
  Chester. What, Richmond, will you prove a runaway?
  Richmond. From thee good Chester? now, the lord
  defend!
Bruce, we will stay and fight.
  Bruce. 'Tis to no end :
We have but twenty men, and they be tired.
But ere we do retire, tell me, Lord Hubert,
Where are my wife and son?

---

* The 4to. reads "Enter or above Hugh, Winchester." *Enter or above* means, that they may either enter on the stage, or stand above on the battlements, as may suit the theatre. With regard to the names *Hugh* and *Winchester*, they are both wrong : they ought to be *Hubert* and *Chester* who have been left by the king to " keep good watch :" when, too, afterwards, Chester asks,
  " What, Richmond, will you prove a runaway?"
The answer in the old copy is—
  " From thee good *Winchester*? now, the lord defend !"
 It ought to be—
  " From thee good *Chester*? now the lord defend !"
and it is clear that the measure requires it. The names throughout are very incorrectly given, and probably the printer composed from a copy in which some alterations had been made in the *dramatis personæ,* but incompletely. Hence the perpetual confusion of *Salisbury* and *Oxford.*

Hubert. Your wife is here; your son we cannot find.
Bruce. Let son and wife, high heavens, your comfort
    find!   [*Exeunt.*

SCENE III.*

   Enter KING, MOWBRAY, LADY BRUCE.
Chester. Bruce hath been here, my lord.
King. I, let him go;
We have good pledges: though we see but one,
The other we are sure will come anon.
   Mowbray. I do advise you, for your own discharge,
Deliver up your son unto the king.
   King. Nay, let her chuse. Come hither, Mowbray.
                    [*The King and Mowbray whisper.*
   Hubert. The King is angry: Lady Bruce, advise you.
   Lady Bruce. What! be advis'd by thee
To have my loving kind and pretty boy,
Given to an unkind killer of sweet boys?
   Chester. Madam, go to; take counsel of your friends.
I warrant you the king will use him well.
   Lady Bruce. I, as he us'd his nephew, Arthur, Ches-
      ter.
God bless my child from being used so!
   Mowbray. Sir Hubert, what are all the people
      voided,
The horses and the cattle turned forth?
   Hubert. Mowbray, they be
   Mowbray. Then will I do the king's commandement.
   Lady Bruce. What will he do? good lord! what will
      he do?
Mowbray, I pray you, what is't you will do?
   Mowbray. Why, fire the castle.
   Lady Bruce. The castle, Mowbray? tarry, tarry,
      man!
Hold me not Chester! gentle Mowbray stay!
Good Hubert, let me go!
   Mowbray. You must not go:
The king is mov'd, and will not hear you speak.

* The scene changes from the outside to the inside of the castle.

Lady Bruce. But he shall hear me! pity me, king
    John!
Call Mowbray back: hear me for pity's sake!
Regard the Lady Bruce's woeful cry!
    King. What dost thou ask?
    Lady Bruce. First call back Mowbray.
    King. Stay, Mowbray. Now, be brief.
    Lady Bruce. I have some linen garments, jewels,
        'tires,
Pack'd in a hamper here within the lodge:
Oh, let me save it from consuming fire!
    King. And is this all?
    Lady Bruce. It's all the little all I here have left.
    King. Away! set fire! linen and trash!
    Lady Bruce. Once more hear me! there's a precious
        gem,
You have not any richer in all the realm:
If fire do blemish it, art never more
To his true colour can the same restore.
    King. Fetch it.
Two of ye help her with her hamper hither.
    Lady Bruce. Nay, nay, one will suffice: the jewel
        if I save,
Is all I ask.   [*Exit with Chester.*
    King. We shall her jewel have.
    Hubert. She is very fearful I should keep her son.
    Lady Bruce. [*Within.*] Ye do, ye do!
    King. Alas, good lady! hark: Chester and she are
        chiding.
        Enter CHESTER *and she, leading the boy.*
    Lady Bruce. Let go his hand! Is this a paw, think
        you,
To hold a tender hand in? fie for shame!
A nobleman so churlish! Look, I pray,
His arms are gristles.
    King. How now, Lady Bruce!
Doth Chester hurt the jewel of your joy?
Now, by my troth, it is a pretty boy?
    Lady Bruce. I; knew your majesty as much as I,
You would say more.
    King. Well, he and you of us no wrong shall have,

But stay in Windsor Castle with Sir Walter Blunt,
And honorably be us'd; provided still,
Your husband and your son obey our will.

    Lady Bruce. For this great mercy, if they disobey,
Myself will chide them. Fortune follow John,
And on his foes fall swift destruction!

    King. Come! let us now after the Queen and Salis-
        bury.   [*Exeunt omnes.*

SCENE IV.

    Enter the QUEEN, SALISBURY, *Soldiers.*
    Queen. Now are ye, worthy and resolved men,
Come to the cage where the unclean birds bide,
That tire* on all the fair flight in the realm.
Summon this castle, or (to keep my words)
This cage of night-hid owls light-flying birds—
                          [*Offer to summon.*
    Enter YOUNG BRUCE, MATILDA, *Soldiers.*
    Salisbury. Stay drum! thou needst not summon
        willing men,
Or rather wilfull; for such methinks they be.

    Queen. See ye yon baggage, muffled in black weeds:
Those clouds fold in the comet that portends
Sad desolation to this royal realm.
For ever seek to mask her light, good friends:
Let us disrobe her of each little beam,
And then your Phœbus will one Phœbe have,
That while they live shall lend your land true light,
Give joy unto your day, rest to your night.
Assail them! stay not.

    Salisbury. Stay, and assay them first!
I say to you, fair Queen, this fact is foul.
Let not provoking words whet dull-edg'd swords,
But try if we can blunt sharp blades with words.
Fitzwater's nephew, Bruce, I see thee there,
And tell thee it is shame for such a boy
To lead a many able men to fight.
And, modest looking maid, I see you too:

---

    * To *tire* is a term in falconry: from the Fr. *tirer,* in reference to
birds of prey tearing what they take to pieces.

An unfit sight to view virginity
Guarded with other soldiers than good prayers.
But you will say the king occasions it:
Say what you will, no king but would take cause
Of just offence.
Yield you, young Bruce, your mother is in hold.
Yield you, young maid, your father is in hold.

   Matilda. Will the queen keep me from the lustful
      king?
Then will I yield.

   Queen. A plague upon this counterfeiting quean.

   Matilda. God's blessed mercy! will you still be mad,
And wrong a noble virgin with vile speech?

   Salisbury. Let me alone. Matilda, maiden fair,
Thou virgin spouse, true Huntington's just heir,
Wilt thou come hither? and I do protest,
The Queen, and I to mitigate this war
Will do what thou would'st have.

   Matilda. I come.

   Bruce. You shall not go. Sound, drums, to war!

   Salisbury. Alack, alack, for woe!
Well, God for us, sith it will needs be so.

                   [Alarum, fight, stay.

   Salisbury. What stay you for?

   Bruce. Matilda's cries do stay us.

   Matilda. Salisbury, I come in hope of thy defence.

   Bruce. First will I die, ere you shall yield yourself
To any coward lord that serves the king.

   Salisbury. Coward, proud boy! Thou find'st me no
      such beast,
And thou shalt rue in earnest this rude jest.

   *[Fight again. Matilda taken, led by the hair by two
      Soldiers.*

   Salisbury. Rude hands! how hale you virtuous honor
      forth!
You do not well: away!
Now by my faith, ye do not well, I say.
Take her, fair queen, use her as she deserves:
She's fair, she's noble, chaste and debonnair.
I must, according to due course of war,

See that our soldiers scatter not too far,
Lest what care won our negligence may lose.   [*Exit.*

   Queen. Is this the Helen, this the paragon,
That makes the English Ilion* flame so fast?

   Matilda. I am not she; you see I am not she:
I am not ravish'd yet, as Helen was.
I know not what will come of John's desire,
That rages like the sea, that burns like fire.

   Queen. Plain John, proud Joan? I'll tear your
      painted face.
Thus, thus I'll use you.

Enter SALISBURY.

   Matilda. Do, do, what you will.

   Salisbury. How goes this geer? ha! foul fall so foul
      a deed!
Poor chaste child of Fitzwater, dost thou bleed?
By God's blest mother! this is more than need;
And more, I tell you true, than I would bear,
Were not the danger of the camp so near.

Enter a MESSENGER.

   Messenger. My lord, the foes have gathered head:
Lord Bruce, the father, joineth with the son.

   Salisbury. Why, here's the matter: we must spend
      our time
To keep your nails from scratching innocence,
Which should have been bestow'd for our defence.
What shall we now do? Help me, holy God!
The foe is come, and we are out of rank.

      [*Skirmish: Queen taken, Matilda rescued.*

Enter OLD BRUCE wounded, led by his Son, and LEI-
CESTER.

   Bruce. Is the field our's?

   Young Bruce. I, thanks to noble Leicester.

   Bruce. Give God thanks, son: be careful to thy
      mother;
Commend me to Fitzwater; love thy brother,
If either arms, or prayers may him recover. [*Falls down.*

   Leicester. How cheers old Bruce?

* The 4to. prints Ilion, Ilinnus.

Young Bruce. His soul to joy is fled,
His grief is in my bosom buried.
    Leicester. His life was dearly bought; for my eyes
        saw
A shambles of dead men about his feet,
Sent by his sword unto eternal shade.
With honor bury him. Cease tears, good Bruce.
    Young Bruce. Tears help not, I confess, yet must I
        weep.
Soldiers, you help to bear him to my tent.
                          [*Exeunt cum Bruce.*
        Enter QUEEN *and* MATILDA.
    Matilda. Be comforted, great Queen : forget my
        wrongs.
It was my fortune, and no fault of your's.
    Queen. Is she thus mild? or doth she mock my
        chance?
    Leicester. Queen Isabel,* are you a prisoner?
See what it is to be a soldier.
But what foul hand hath harm'd Matilda's fair?
Speak, honourable maid, who tore thy hair?
Did Salisbury or the Queen this violence?
    Matilda. Ungentle grooms first took and tore me
        thus,
From whom old Salisbury, chastising their wrong,
Most kindly brought me to this gentle queen ;
Who laid her soft hand on my bleeding cheeks,
Gave kisses to my lips, wept for my woe;
And was devising how to send me back,
Even when your last alarum frighted us,
And by her kindness fell into your hands.
    Leicester. Which kindness we return: Madam, be
        free.
Soldiers, conduct the Queen whither she please.
    Queen. Farewell Matilda : if I live, believe,
I will remember this. Oh, how I grieve,
That I should wrong so innocent a maid !

---

   * The 4to. has it *Elinor*, but it ought to be *Isabel*. The previous
entrance of the Queen and Matilda is not marked.

Come, lady, old Fitzwater is not far:
He'll weep to see these scars, full well I know.
  Matilda. Would I were from this woeful world of
      war !
Sure I will 'scape and to some nunnery go.   [*Exeunt.*

SCENE V.

Enter KING, SALISBURY, HUBERT.
  King. Had you her, then, had you her in your power?
  Salisbury. I, marry, had we: we had taken her.
  King. Oh, had she been in mine, not all earth's power
From my power should have freed her !
  Salisbury. You are a king, and high are princes'
      thoughts :
It may be, with your sight you could have chas'd
A host of armed men ; it may be so :
But we, your subjects, did the best we could.
Yet Bruce the father, backing Bruce the son,
Scatter'd our troops, brought rescue to Matilda,
And took your peerless queen their prisoner.
  King. On all the race of Bruces for this wrong
I will have vengeance ! Hubert, call in Brand,
                              [*Exit Hubert.*
My lord of Salisbury, give us leave awhile
To be alone.
  Salisbury. I will my liege. Be you comforted ;
The Queen will be recovered, do not fear,
As well as e'er she was.
  King. Salisbury, forbear I pray.
  Salisbury. Yet for the wrong she did unto Matilda,
I fear, I fear.——   [*Exit.*
  King. The father and the son did rescue her ;
The mother and the son shall rue the deed.
So it shall be ; I am resolv'd thereon.
Matilda, my souls food, those have bereft,
And these of body's food I will bereave.
              Enter HUBERT, BRAND.
  King. Will Brand.

Brand. Your Majesty. [*Make legs.*

King. Less of your court'sy. Hubert, stand aside.
Post speedily to Windsor; take this ring;
Bid Blunt deliver Bruce's wife and child
Into your hands, and ask him for the key
Of the dark tower o'er the dungeon vault:
In that, see you shut up the dam and brat.
Pretend to Blunt that you have left them meat,
Will serve some s'ennight; and unto him say,
It is my will you bring the key away.
And hear you, sir, I charge you on your life,
You do not leave a bit of bread with them.

Brand. I warrant you; let me alone.

King. Come back again with all the speed you may.
[*Exit. Brand.*

Hubert. Some cruel task is pointed for that slave,
Which he will execute as cruelly.

King. No ruth, no pity shall have harbour here,
Till fair Matilda be within these arms.

Enter SALISBURY *with the* QUEEN.

Salisbury. Comfort, my lord; comfort, my gracious
lord;
Your love is come again!

King. Ah, Salisbury, where?

Salisbury. Here, my dread sovereign.

King. Thou liest, she is not there.

Salisbury. Under correction you wrong my age.
Say, I beseech you, is not this the Queen?

King. I cry you mercy, Salisbury; 'tis indeed.
Where is Matilda?

Queen. Where virtue, chastity, and innocence remain;
There is Matilda.

King. How comes she, pray, to be so chaste, so fair,
So virtuous in your eye?

Queen. She freed me from my foes, and never urg'd
My great abuse when she was prisoner.

King. What did you to her?

Queen. Rail'd upon her first,
Then tare her hair and rent her tender cheeks.

King. Oh heaven! was not the day dark at that
    foul deed?
Could the sun see without a red eclipse
The purple tears fall from those tyrant wounds?
Out Ethiop, Gypsy, thick-lipp'd blackamoor!
Wolf, tigress! worse than either of them both!
    Salisbury. Are you advis'd, my lord?
    King. Out, doting Earl!
Could'st thou endure to see such violence,
    Salisbury. I tell you plain, my lord, I brook'd it not,
But stay'd the tempest.
    King. Rend my love's cheeks! that matchless effigy,
Of wonder-working nature's chiefest work:
Tear her rich hair! to which gold wires,
Suns' rays, and best of best compares
(In their most pride) have no comparison.
Abuse her name! Matilda's sacred name!
Oh, barbarous outrage, rudeness merciless!
    Queen. I told you, Salisbury, you mistook the king.
    Salisbury. I did indeed. My liege lord, give me
    leave
To leave the camp.
    King. Away old fool! and take with thee that trull;
For if she stay——
    Salisbury. Come, lady, come away,
Tempt not his rage. Ruin wrath always brings:
Lust being lord, there is no trust in kings.   [*Exeunt.*
       Enter MOWBRAY.
    Mowbray. To arms king John! Fitzwater's field is
    pitch'd,
About some mile hence on a champain plain.
Chester hath drawn our soldiers in array:
The wings already have begun the fight.
    King. Thither we will with wings of vengeance fly,
And win Matilda, or lose victory!   [*Exeunt.*

ACT IV. SCENE I.

Enter LADY BRUCE *and her* BOY *with* BRAND.

Lady Bruce. Why did my keeper put us in thy
      hands?
Wherein have we offended Blunt or thee?
  Brand. You need not make these words:
You must remove your lodging; this is all.
Be not afeard: come, come, here is the door.
  Lady Bruce. Oh God, how dark it is!
  Brand. Go in, go in: it's higher up the stairs.
  Lady Bruce. My trembling heart forbids me to go
      in.
Oh, if thou have compassion, tell me true,
What my poor boy and I must trust unto?
  Brand. I tell thee true, compassion is my foe;
Yet have I had of thee compassion.
Take in thy child: as I have faith or troth,
Thou and thy boy shall be but prisoners,
And I must daily bring you meat and drink.
  Lady Bruce. Well, thou hast sworn, and God so
      give thee light
As in this dark place thou rememb'rest us.
Poor heart, thou laugh'st, and hast not wit to think
Upon the many fears that me afflict.
I will not in.   Help us, assist us, Blunt!
We shall be murdered in a dungeon!
  Brand. Cry without cause? I'll have ye in, i'faith.
  Lady Bruce. Oh, let my boy and I but dine with
      Blunt,
And then I will with patience go in.
  Brand. Will ye, or nill ye, zounds! ye must go in,
And never dine.
  Lady Bruce. What say'st thou? never dine!
  Brand. No, not with Blunt I mean.   Go in, I say;
Or, by this hand, ye get no meat to day.
  Lady Bruce. My child is hungry: when shall he
      have meat?
  Brand. Why, and ye would go in, immediately.

Lady Bruce. I will go in; but very much I doubt,
Nor I, nor my poor boy shall e'er come out.   [*Exeunt.*
                                   [*He seems to lock a door.*
   Brand. Ne'er while ye live, i'faith! now are they sure.
Cry till their hearts ache no man can them hear.
A miserable death is famishment;
But what care I? The king commanded me.

SCENE II.

Alarum within: excursions: Enter FITZWATER,
                   BRUCE.
   Fitzwater. Now   doth fair fortune offer hope of
        speed;
But howsoe'er we speed, good cousin Bruce,
March with three hundred bows and pikes to Windsor,
Spreading a rumour that the day is our's,
As ours it shall be with the help of heaven.
Blunt loves our part far better than the king's,
And will, I gage my life, upon the news
Surrender up the castle to our use.
By this means shall you help us to a hold,
Howe'er it chance: set free your lady mother,
That lives in prison there with your young brother.
   Bruce. Away, good uncle, to the battle go!
But that a certain good ensues, I know,
For all the world I would not leave you so.
   Fitzwater. Away, away!
God send thee Windsor; us this happy day.
   Alarum still.   Enter HUBERT *and* MATILDA.*
   Hubert. You cannot hide yourself, Matilda; no dis-
        guise
Will serve the turn: now must you to the king,
And all these wars will with your presence cease.
Yield you to him, he soon will yield to peace.
   Matilda. They say thou took'st some pity of a child,
The king appointing thee to sear his eyes:
Men do report thee to be just of word,

   * Matilda's name is omitted in the old copy, but the errors of
this kind are too numerous to be always pointed out.

And a dear lover of my lord the king.
If thou didst that, if thou be one of these,
Pity Matilda prostrate at thy feet.

Hubert. I sav'd young Arthur's eyes, and pity thee;
My word is just, which I have given the king;
The king I love, and thee I know he loves:
Compare these, then how can I pleasure thee?

Matilda. By letting me escape to Dunmow Abbey,
Where I will end my life a votary.

Hubert. And the king die with doting on thy love.

Matilda. No, no: this fire of lust would be soon
　　laid,
If once he knew me sworn a holy maid.

Hubert. Thy tears and love of virtue have the power
To make me at an instant true and false:
True to distressed beauty and rare chastity;
False to king John, that holds the sight of thee
Dearer than England or earth's empery.
Go, happy soul, that in so ill an age
Hast such fair beauty for thy heritage:
Yet go not so alone.   Dost hear, tall soldier?
　　　　　　　　　　　　　[*Call a Soldier.*
I know thee honest: guide this gentle maid,
To Dunmow Abbey: she is one I know.
I will excuse thee and content thee well.
My signet take, that ye may pass unsearch'd.

Matilda. Kind Hubert, many prayers for this good
　　deed
Shall on my beads be daily number'd.　　[*Exeunt.*
　　Enter LEICESTER, RICHMOND, FITZWATER.

Leicester. Oh, treble heat of honor, toil and rage!
How cheers earl Richmond? Fitzwater, speak old man.
We are now near together: answer me.

Fitzwater. Leicester, the more our woe;
The likelier to be taken by the foe.

Richmond. Oh, let not such a thought abuse thy age!
We'll never yield us to the tyrant's rage.

Leicester. But if my girl be yielded—

Leicester. If she be?

Fitzwater. I, I:

There's no man but shall have his time to die.

Leicester. Now is our hour, which they shall dearly
    buy.

Enter KING, HUBERT, CHESTER, MOWBRAY.

Richmond. Leicester, we'll stand like three battalions :
What says our noble general thereto ?

Fitzwater. Why, I say do :
While I can, I'll keep my place with you.

King. How now, my bug-bear, will you now submit ?

Leicester. To death, but not to thee.

King. Richmond, nor you ?

Richmond. Earl Richmond will not yield.

King. Methinks, Fitzwater, you should have more wit.

Fitzwater. If it be wit to live, I have no will ;
And so in this my will o'errules my wit.

King. Alarum then ! with weapons will we scourge
Your desperate will, and teach ye to have wit.

                    [*Fight: drive back the King.*

King. Of high heroic spirits be they all.
We will withdraw a little and confer,
For they are circled round, and cannot 'scape.

                              [*withdraw.*

Richmond. Oh, that we three, who in the sun's arise
Were, like the three Triumvirates * of Rome,
Guides of an host, able to vanquish Rome,
Are now alone, enclos'd with enemies!

Fitzwater. The glory of the world hath no more stay,
But as it comes, it fleets, and fades away.

Leicester. Courage, and let us die ! they come again :
It's Lord Hubert alone. Hubert, what news ? †

                Enter HUBERT.

Hubert. This day's fierce slaughter, John, our king,
    laments,
And to you three, great leaders of an host,

---

* The author probably wrote " *Triumviri* of Rome."
† Nothing can more clearly shew the desperate confusion of
names in this play than this line, which in the 4to. stands,
    " It's lord *Hugh Burgh* alone: *Hughberr,* what news ?"
In many places Hubert is only called *Hugh.*

That now have not a man at all to lead,
You, worthy captains without companies—
    Leicester. Fitzwater! Richmond! by the blessed sun,
Lord Hubert mocks us.
    Hubert. By the moon, I do not; and put the blessed
        to't,
It is as good an oath as you have sworn.
My heart grieves, that so great hearts as yours be,
Should put your fortunes on a sort* of slaves,
That bring base fear within them to the field.
But to the matter.   Sith your state is such,
That without mercy you are sure of death,
(Which I am sure, and well his highness knows,
You do not fear at all) yet he gives grant,
On just conditions you shall save your lives.
    Fitzwater. On no condition will I save my life,
Except Matilda be return'd aguin,
Unblemish'd, unabus'd; and then I yield.
    Hubert. She now is where she never will return.
    Fitzwater. Never? Oh God! Is my Matilda dead?
    Hubert. Dead to the world; dead to this woe she is.
She lives at Dunmow, and is vow'd a nun.
    Fitzwater. Do not delude me, Hubert, gentle son.
    Hubert. By all the faith and honor of my kin,
By my unstain'd allegiance to the king,
By my own word, that hath reproveless been,
She is at Dunmow.
    Fitzwater. Oh, how came she there?
    Hubert. When all these fields were walks for rage
        and fear
(This, howling like a head of hungry wolves,†
That, scudding as a herd of frighted deer)
When dust, arising like a coal black fog,
From friend divided friend, join'd foe to foe,
Yet neither those, nor these could either know;

---

* *Sort* is company or collection: See note to p. 21. of *the Down-fall of Huntington.*

† " *Head* of hungry wolves," is the reading of the original copy:
a " *herd* of hungry wolves" would scarcely be proper, but it may
have been so written.

Till here and there, through large wide-mouthed wounds
Proud life, even in the glory of his heat,
Losing possession, belch'd forth streams of blood,
Whose spouts in falling made ten thousand drops,
And with that purple shower the dust alaid:
At such a time met I the trembling maid;
Seeming a dove from all her fellows parted,
Seen, known, and taken; unseen and unknown,
To any other that did know us both.
At her entreats I sent her safely guided
To Dunmow Abbey; and the guide return'd
Assures me she was gladfully receiv'd,
Pitied, and in his sight did take her oath.
  Fitzwater. Hubert, for this thy honourable deed,
I and my house will reverence thy name.
  Hubert. Yet, I beseech you, hide it from the king;
At least, that I convey'd her to the place.
    Enter KING, MOWBRAY, CHESTER.
  Fitzwater. Hubert I will.
  King. What, stand they still on terms?
  Leicester. On honourable terms, on terms of right.
Our lives without our liberty we scorn.
  King. You shall have life and liberty, I swear.
  Leicester. Then, Leicester bows his knee to his liege
    lord,
And humbly begs his highness to beware
Of wronging innocence, as he hath done.
  Richmond. The like Richmond desires, and yields
    his sword.
  King. I do embrace ye both, and hold myself
Richer by a whole realm in having you.
  Fitzwater. Much is my wrong; yet I submit with
    these,
Begging free leave to live a private life.
  King. Old brands of malice in thy bosom rest:
Thou shalt have leave to leave me, never doubt.
Fitzwater, see thou ship thee strait for France,
And never set thy foot on English shore,
Till I repeal thee. Go; go hence in peace.
  Leicester. Why doth your highness wrong Fitzwater
    thus?

King. I right his wrong : he's weary of the land.
Richmond. Not of the land, but of a public life.
King. Content ye lords : in such quick times as these
We must not keep a drone among our bees.
Fitzwater. I am as glad to go, as you to send :
Yet I beseech this favour of your Grace,
That I may see Matilda ere I part.
King. Matilda! see Matilda, if thou canst,
Before sunset : stay not another day.
Fitzwater.* The Abbey walls, that shroud my happy
        child,
Appear within her hapless father's sight.
Farewell my sovereign, Leicester, Richmond, Lords;
Farewell to all : grief gives no way to words.
King. Fitzwater stay : lords, give us leave awhile.
Hubert, go you before unto the abbess,
And signify our coming. Let her bring,
Matilda to her father. *(Exit Hubert.)* Come, old
        man ;
Be not too froward, and we shall be friends.
About this girl our mortal jars began,
And, if thou wilt, here all our quarrel ends.
Fitzwater. Reserve my honour, and my daughter's
        fame,
And no poor subject that your grace commands
Shall willinger submit, obey, and serve.
King. Do then but this. Persuade thy beauteous
        child
To leave the nunnery and return to court,
And I protest from henceforth to forswear
All such conceits of lust as I have borne.
Fitzwater. I will, my lord, do all that I may do ;
But give me leave, in this, to doubt of you.
King. This small thing grant, and ask me any thing ;
Or else die in exile, loath'd of the king.
Fitzwater. You shall perceive I will do what I may.

* In the old copy the four following lines are given to king John.

Enter, on the wall, ABBESS, MATILDA. *Re-enter*
HUBERT.

Hubert. Matilda is afraid to leave the house;
But lo, on yonder battlement she stands,
But in no case will come within your hands.

King. What! will my lady abbess wars with us?
Speak, lady; wherefore shut you up your gates?

Abbess. Have we not reason, when an host of men
Hunt and pursue religious chastity?
King John, bethink thee what thou tak'st in hand,
On pain of interdiction of thy land.
Murderers and felons may have sanctuary,
And shall not honorable maids distress'd,
Religious virgins, holy nuns profess'd,
Have that small privilege? Now, out upon thee, out!
Holy saint Catherine, shield my virginity!
I never stood in such extremity.

Hubert. My lord, the abbess lies, I warrant you;
For I have heard there is a monk of Bury,
That once a week comes thither to make merry.

King. Content thee, Hubert; that same monk and
     she,
And the worst come, my instruments shall be.
Good lady abbess, fear no violence:
There's not one here shall offer you offence.

Fitzwater. Daughter, all this while tears my speech
     have staid.
My lord the king, lords all draw near, I pray,
And hear a poor man's parting from his child.
Matilda, still my unstain'd honor's joy,
Fair ornament of old Fitzwater's coat,
Born to rich fortunes, did not this ill age
Bereave thee of thy birthright's heritage,
Thou see'st our sovereign, lord of both our lives,
A long besieger of thy chastity,
Hath scatter'd all our forces, slain our friends,
Razed our castles, left us ne'er a house
Wherein to hide us from his wrathful eye:
Yet God provides; France is appointed me,
And thou find'st house-room in this nunnery.

Here, if the king should doat as he hath done,
It's sacrilege to tempt a holy nun :
But I have hope, he will not ; yet my fear
So drowns my hope, as I am forced to stay,
And leave abruptly what I more would say.
   Matilda. Oh, go not yet, my griev'd heart's com-
      forter !
I am as valiant to resist desire
As ever thou wert worthy in the field.
John may attempt, but if Matilda yield,
Oh then——
   Fitzwater. I, then, Matilda, thou dost lose
The former glory of thy chaste resolves.
These seven years hast thou bid* a martyr's pains,
Resisting in thyself lust-growing fire,
For being mortal sure thou hast desire ;
And five sad winters have their full course run,
Since thou didst bury noble Huntington.
In these years, many months, and many days
Have been consum'd thy virtues to consume.
Gifts have been heralds ; pandars did presume
To tempt thy chaste ears, with their unchaste tongues :
All, in effect, working to no effect :
For I was still the watchman of thy tower,
The keeper of foul worms from my fair flower.
But now, no more, no more Fitzwater may
Defend his poor lamb from the lion's prey ;
Thy order and thy holy prayers may.
To help thee thou hast privilege by law ;
Therefore be resolute, and nobly die !
Abhor base lust, defend thy chastity.
   King. Despatch, Fitzwater : hinder not thy child :
Many preferments do on her await.
   Fitzwater. I, girl ; I know thou shall be offer'd
      wealth
(Which is a shrewd enticement in sad want)
Great honors to lift up thy low estate,
And glorious titles to eternize thee.

   † *Bid* is used here, and often in old writers, for *invited.*

All these do but gild over ugly shame;
Such wealth, my child, foreruns releaseless need,
Such honor ever proves dishonorate.
For titles, none comes near a virtuous name:
Oh keep it ever, as thou hast done yet !
And though these dark times should forget thy praise,
An age will come, that shall eternize it.
Bid me farewell, and speak it in a word.
  Matilda. Farewell, dear father.
  Fitzwater. Oh, farewell, sweet child.
My liege farewell: Leicester, Richmond, Hubert,
Chester and Mowbray, friends and foes, farewell.
Matilda, see thou keep thy spotless fame,
And live eterniz'd, else die soon with shame.   [*Exit.*
  Matilda. Amen, amen : father, adieu, adieu!
Grief dwells with me, sweet comfort follow you.
  Abbess. Come, daughter, come. This is a woeful sight,
When good endeavors are oppress'd by might.
                [*Exeunt from above, Abbess, Matilda.*
  King. Ah, Hubert, seest thou not the sun go down,
Cloudy and dark ? Matilda, stay ! one word.
She shakes her head, and scornfully says nay.
  Richmond. How cheer'st thou Leicester ?
  Leicester. Mad, man, at my state,
That cannot raise true honor ruinate.
                Enter MESSENGER.
  King. I will not be disdain'd. I vow to see
Quick vengeance on this girl for scorning me.
  Messenger. Young Bruce, my lord, hath gotten Wind-
        sor castle,
Slain Blunt your constable, and those that kept it;
And finding in a tower his mother dead,
With his young brother starv'd and famished,
That every one may see the rueful sight,
In the thick wall he a wide window makes;
And as he found them, so he lets them be,
A spectacle to every comer by,
That heaven and earth, your tyrant shame may see.
All people cursing, crying fie upon
The tyrant, merciless inhuman John.

King. Chester and Mowbray, march away to Windsor :
Suppress that traitor Bruce.   What if his dam,
In wilful fury, would receive no meat,
Nor suffer her young child any to eat,
Is it our fault ? haste ye with speed away,
And we will follow. Go ; begone, I pray.
                     [*Exeunt. Chester, Mowbray.*
Hubert. Oh black and woeful deed ! oh, piteous thing,
When slaves attend the fierce thoughts of a king.
Leicester. My lord, shall we go too ?
King. Leicester and Richmond, I ; I pray ye do.
Leicester. Get I my bear and ragged staff * once more
Rais'd in the field, for these wrongs some shall roar.
                     [*Exeunt Richmond, Leicester.*
King. Fetch in the monk of Bury, that I talk'd of,
                     [*Exit Hubert, for the monk.*
And bid Will Brand, my instrument of death,
Come likewise in. Convert to raging hate,
          Enter MONK, HUBERT, BRAND.
My long-resisted love ! welcome, good Monk.
Monk. Thanks to my liege.
King. Thou hast been long in suit
To be installed abbot of your house,
And in your favour many friends have stirr'd.
Now is the hour that you shall be preferr'd,
Upon condition, and the matter small.
Short shrift to make, good honest confessor,
I love a fair nun, now in Dunmow abbey :
The abbess loves you, and you pleasure her ;
Now if between you two, this pretty lady
Could be persuaded to affect a king,
Your suit is granted, and on Dunmow abbey
I will bestow a hundred marks a year.
  Monk. A holy nun ! a young nun, and a lady !
Dear ware, my lord ; yet bid you well as may be.
Strike hands ; a bargain : she shall be your own,
Or if she will not—
King. Nay, if she do refuse,
I'll send a death's man with you ; this is he.

* See the *The Downfall of Huntington*, note to p. 69.

If she be wilful, leave her to his hands,
And on her own head be her hasted end.
   Monk. The matter shall be done.
   King. Sirrah, what poisons have you ready ?
   Brand. Store, store.
   King. Wait on the monk, then, and ere we take horse,
I'll give you such instructions as you need.
Hubert, prepare to Windsor with our host.
                 [Exeunt King, Monk, and Brand.
   Hubert. Your tyrannies have lost my love almost,
And yet I cannot chuse but love eternally
This wanton king, replete with cruelty.
Oh ! how are all his princely virtues stain'd
With lust, abhorred, and lascivious heat,
Which kindling first to fire, now in a flame
Shews to the whole world clearly his foul shame.
To quench this flame full many a tide of tears,
Like overflowing-full seas, have been spent ;
And many a dry land drunk with human blood ;
Yet nothing helps his passions violent :
Rather, they add oil to his raging fire,
Heat to his heat, desire to his desire.
Somewhat, I fear, is now a managing,
For that prodigious bloody stigmatic*
Is never call'd unto his kingly sight,
But like a comet he portendeth still
Some innovation, or some monstrous act,
Cruel, unkindly, horrid, full of hate;
As that vile deed at Windsor done of late.
Gentle Matilda, somewhat I mistrust ;

   * This word is found in Henry the VI, part ii. act v. sc. 1, where
young Clifford applies it to Richard. Malone observes in a note,
that according to Bullokar's *English Expositor*, 1616, *stygmatick* originally and properly signified " a person who has been *branded* with a
hot iron for some crime." The name of the man to whom Hubert here
applies the word, is *Brand.*
   Webster in his *Vittoria Corombona* (D. O. P. VI. 264) applies the
term metaphorically.
        " The god of melancholy turn thy gall to poison
         And let the *stigmatic* wrinkles in thy face,
         Like to the boisterous waves in a rough tide,
         One still overtake another."

Yet thee I need not fear, such is his love.
Again, the place doth give thee warrantize ;
Yet I remember when his highness said,
The lustful monk of Bury should him aid.
I, so it is : if she have any ill,
Through the lewd shaveling will her shame be wrought.
If it so chance, Matilda's guiltless wrong
Will with the loss of many a life be bought.
But Hubert will be still his dread lord's friend,
However he deserves, his master serve ;
Though he neglect, him will I not neglect :
Whoever fails him, I will John affect ;
For though kings fault in many a foul offence,
Subjects must sue, not mend with violence.   [*Exit.*

SCENE III.

Enter OXFORD, QUEEN.

Oxford. Now, by my faith, you are to blame, madam,
Ever tormenting, ever vexing you :
Cease of these fretting humours, pray ye do.
Grief will not mend it ; nought can pleasure you,
But patient suffering ; nor, by your grace's leave,
Have you such cause to make such hue and cry
After a husband ; you have not in good sooth.
Yearly a child ! this payment is not bad.
Content, fair queen, and do not think it strange,
That Kings do sometimes seek delight in change :
For now and then, I tell you, poor men range.
Sit down a little, I will make you smile.
Though I be now like to the snowy Alps,
I was as hot as Ætna in my youth ;
All fire, i'faith, true heart of oak, right steel,
A ruffian, lady. Often for my sport
I to a lodge of mine did make resort,
To view my deer, I said ; dear God can tell,
It was my keeper's wife whom I lov'd well.
My countess, (God be with her) was a shrow,
As women be, your majesty doth know ;
And some odd pick-thank put it in her head,
All was not well : but such a life I led,

And the poor keeper and his smooth-fac'd wife,
That will I, nill I, there she might not bide.
But for the people I did well provide;
And, by God's mother, for my lady's spite,
I trick'd her in her kind, I serv'd her right.
Were she at Londou, I the country kept;
Come thither, I at London would sojourn;
Came she to court, from court I straightway stept;
Return, I to the court would back return.
So this way, that way, every way she went,
I still was retrograde, seld* opposite:
Till at the last, by mildness and submission,
We met, kiss'd, join'd, and here left all suspicion.

    Queen. Now out upon you, Vere: I would have
        thought,
The world had not contain'd a chaster man.

    Oxford. Now, by my fay, I will be sworn I am.
In all I tell you I confess no ill,
But that I curb'd a froward woman's will:
Yet had my keeper's wife been of my mind,
There had been cause some fault with us to find;
But I protest, her noes and nays were such,
That for my life she ever kept go much.

    Queen. You would take nay, but our king John says no;
No nay, no answer will suffice his turn:
He, for he cannot tempt true chastity,
Fills all the land with hostile cruelty.
Is it not shame, he that should punish sin,
Defend the righteous, help the innocent,
Carves with his sword the purpose of his will,
Upon the guarders of the virtuous,
And hunts admired spotless maidenhead
With all the darts of desolation,
Because she scorneth to be dissolute?
Me, that he leaves, I do not murmur at;
That he loves her doth no whit me perplex,

---

  * The sense seems to require that we should read
      "I still was retrogade, *still* opposite;"
unless Oxford mean that he seldom met his wife face to face, but
kept out of her way.

If she did love him, or myself did hate:
But this alone is it that doth me vex;
He leaves me that loves him, and her pursues,
That loaths him and loves me.   How can I chuse
But sadly grieve, and mourn in my green youth,
When nor of her, nor me he taketh ruth?
   Oxford. Ha' done, good Queen; for God's good love,
      ha' done:
This raging humor will no doubt be staid.
Virtuous Matilda is profess'd a nun;
Within a mile, at Dunmow, lives the maid.
God will not suffer any thing so vile;
He will not, sure, that he should her defile.
   Queen. Nor church, nor chapel, abbey, nunnery,
Are privileg'd from his intemperance.
But leave we him, and let us, I entreat,
Go visit fair Matilda: much I am
In debt unto the maid.
   Oxford. You are indeed:
You wrong'd her, when with blows you made her bleed.
But if you please to visit her, fair dame,
Our coach is ready: we will soon be there.
   Queen. Thanks Oxford: and with us I mean to bear,
The beauteous garland sent me out of Spain,
Which I will offer in the Abbey chapel,
As witness of Matilda's chastity;
Whom while I live, I ever vow to love,
In recompence of rash and causeless wrong.

ACT V.   SCENE I.

Enter BRAND *solus; with cup, bottle of poison.*
   Brand. Good, by this hand! exceeding, passing,
      good!
The dog no sooner drank it, but yugh! yugh! quoth he:
So grins me with his teeth, lies down and dies:
Yugh! quoth I: by God's blood, go thy ways.
Of all thy line and generation,
Was never dog so worshipp'd as thou art,
For ere thou died'st thou wert an officer.
I lie not, by these nails: a squire's place;

For the vile cur became a countess' taster :
So died the dog.   Now in our next account
The countess comes; let's see a Countess and a nun :
Why so; why so.
What, would she have the whole world quite undone?
We'll mete* her for that trick.   What, not a king?
Hanging's too good for her.   I am but a plain knave,
And yet should any of these " no forsooths,"
These pray-aways, these trip-and-goes, these tits,
Deny me, now by these—
A plague upon this bottle and this cup,
I cannot act mine oath! but to 't again—
By these ten ends of flesh and blood, I swear,
First with this hand, wound thus about her hair,
And with this dagger lustily lambackt†—
I would, i'faith, I, by my villainy,
I would— But here, but here she comes,
Led by two doctors in sweet lechery.
If they speed, with my poison I go by;
If not, have at you maid; then step in I.

Enter MATILDA, *between the* MONK *and the* ABBESS.‡

   Monk.   And as I said, fair maid, you have done well,
In your distress, to seek this holy place.
But tell me truly, how do you expel
The rage of lust-arising heat in you?
   Matilda.   By prayer, by fasting, by considering
The shame of ill, and meed of doing well.
   Abbess.   But daughter, daughter, tell me in my ear,
Have you no fleshly fightings now and then? [*Whisper.*
   Brand.   Fleshly quoth you? a maid of three score
       years,

---

  * *Mete* here is used in the sense of *match.*

  † *Lambackt*] So the word stands in the original : the sense is
clear, but *lambackt* is not to be found in any glossary or dictionary.
Lambeak'd, in the sense of *struck*, comes nearest to it, and would
render the passage intelligible. Nobody has attempted to give the
etymology of to *lambeake*, but perhaps it was a corruption of *limb-
beat ;* or it may be from *lambo*, to lick, as a *licking* and a *beating*
are synonymous.   The Rev. A. Dyce, the judicious and accurate
editor of Peele's Works, suggests " *I am back'd*" as the correct
reading.

  ‡ The 4to. says, " between the Monk and the *Nun.*"

And fleshly fightings sticking in her teeth?
Well, wench, thou'rt match'd, i'faith.
   Abbess. You do confess the king hath tempted you,
And thinking now and then on gifts and state,
A glowing heat hath proudly puff'd you up:
But thanks to God, his grace hath done you good.
   Monk. Who? the king's grace?
   Matilda. No: God's grace, holy Monk.
   Monk. The king's grace fain would do you good, fair
     maid.
   Matilda. Ill good: he means my fame to violate.
   Abbess. Well, let that be.
   Brand. Good bawd, good mother B.
How fain you would that that good deed should be!
   Abbess. I was about to say somewhat upon a thing:
Oh thus it is.
We maids that all the day are occupied
In labour, and chaste hallow'd exercise,
Are nothing so much tempted while day lasts,
As we are tried and proved in the night.
Tell me, Matilda, had you since you came,
No dreams, no visions, nothing worth the note?
   Matilda. No, I thank God.
   Abbess. Truly you will, you will,
Except you take good heed and bless yourself;
For if I lie but on my back awhile
I am, past recovery, sure of a bad dream.
You see yon reverend Monk: now, God he knows,
I love him dearer for his holiness,
And I believe the devil knows it too;
For the foul fiend comes to me many a night,
As like the Monk, as if he were the man.
Many a hundred nights the Nuns have seen,
Pray, cry, make crosses, do they what they can.
Once gotten in, then do I fall to work,
My holy-water bucket being near hand,
I whisper secret spells, and conjure him,
That the foul fiend hath no more power to stand:
He down, as I can quickly get him laid,
I bless myself, and like a holy maid,

Turn on my right side, where I sleep all night
Without more dreams, or troubling of the sprite.

Brand. An Abbess? By the cross of my good blade,*
An excellent mother to bring up a maid!
For me I mean, and my good master, John;
But never any for an honest man.   [*Coughs.*
Now, fie upon that word of honesty,
Passing my throat 't had almost choked me:
Sblood, I'll forswear it for this trick.

Monk. We trifle time. Fair maid, it's thus in brief:
This Abbey by your means may have relief;
An hundred marks a year.   Answer, I pray,
What will you do herein?

Matilda. Even all I may.

Abbess. It's charitably spoken, my fair child:
A little thing of your's, a little help,
Will serve the turn: learn but to bear, to bear
The burden of this world, and it will do.

Brand. Well, go thy ways: is this no bawd think
        you?

Matilda. Madam, the heavy burden of the world
Hath long oppress'd me.

Abbess. But not 'press'd you right;
Now shall you bear a burden far more light.

Matilda. What burden-bearing? whereto tends this
        talk?

Monk. To you, to us, this Abbey, and king John.

Matilda. Oh, God forefend he should be thought
        upon!

Monk. Lady, make short: the king must lie with you.

Matilda. With me? with me?
        [*First turns to the Monk, then to the Abbess.*

Abbess. Sweet, never look so strange:
He shall come closely,† nobody shall see.

* To swear by the cross of the sword was a very common prac-
tice, and many instances are to be found in D. O. P. but see parti-
cularly note 2, to the *Pinner of Wakefield*, vol. ii. and notes on
Hamlet, A. I. Sc. 5.

† i. e. *secretly*—a very common application of the word in our old
writers. Several examples are collected in a note to *King John*
A. IV. Sc. 1.

Matilda. How can he come, but one hath eyes to
    see?

Monk. Your chamber windows shall be shadowed.

Matilda. But no veil from my conscience shadows
    me.

Abbess. And all the Nuns sent quietly to bed.

Matilda. But they will rise, and by my blushing red,
Quickly give guess of my lost maidenhead.

Brand. She goes, i'faith: by God, she is their own!

Monk. Be not so nice, the sin is venial,
Considering you yield for charity;
And by your fall, the nunnery shall rise.

Abbess. Regard good council, daughter: pray, be
    wise.

Monk. Come, here's a stir! will't do wench? will it
    do?

Abbess. Say I, say I; forget the sound of no,
Or else say no and take it: wilt thou so?

Matilda. Do you intend thus lewdly as you speak?

Brand.* I, by Gog's blood, do they: and, moppet, you
    were best
To take their proffers, lest if they forsake you,
I play the devil's part, step in and take you.

Matilda. Some holy water! help me, blessed Nuns!
Two damned spirits, in religious weeds,
Attempt to tempt my spotless chastity;
And a third devil, gaping for my soul,
With horrid starings ghastly frighteth me.

Abbess. You may
Call while you will; but, maid, list what we say,
Or be assur'd this is your dying day.

Matilda. In his name that did suffer for my sin,
And by this blessed sign, I conjure you.

                              [*Draws a crucifix.*
Depart, foul fiends, and cease to trouble me.

Brand. Zounds, she thinks us devils! Hear you, con-
    juror.

---

* Here, according to what follows, Brand steps forward and
addresses Matilda. Hitherto he has spoken *aside.*

Except you use that trick, to conjure down
The standing spirit of my lord the King,
That your good mother there, the Abbess, uses
To conjure down the spirit of the Monk,
Not all your crosses have the power to bless
Your body from a sharp and speedy death.

Matilda. Are ye not fiends, but mortal bodies, then?
[*Feels them all.*

Brand. Maid, maid, catch lower, when you feel
    young men.
'Sblood, I was never taken for the devil till now.

Matilda. Oh, where shall chastity have true defence,
When churchmen lay this siege to innocence?
Where shall a maid have certain sanctuary,
When Lady Lust rules all the nunnery?
Now fie upon ye both, false seeming saints,
Incarnate devils, devilish hypocrites!
A cowled Monk, an aged veiled Nun,
Become false Pandars, and with lustful speech
Essay the chaste ears of true maidenhead!
Now fie upon this age. Would I were dead!

Monk. Come, leave her, lady: she shall have her wish.

Abbess. Speed her, I pray thee: should the baggage live,
She'll slander all the chaste nuns in the land.
[*Exeunt Monk, Abbess.*

Brand. Well, well, go; get you two unto your con-
    juring:
Let me alone to lay her on God's ground.

Matilda. Why dost thou stay?

Brand. Why, maid, because I must:
I have a message to you from the king.

Matilda. And thou art welcome to his humble maid.
I thought thee to be grim and fierce at first,
But now thou hast a sweet aspect, mild looks.
Art thou not come to kill me from the king?

Brand. Yes.

Matilda. And thou art welcome; even the welcom'st
    man,
That ever came unto a woeful maid.
Be brief good fellow: I have in the world

No goods to give, no will at all to make;
But God's will, and the king's, on me be done.
A little money, kept to give in alms,
I have about me: deaths-man take it all;
Thou art the last poor alms-man I shall see.
Come, come, despatch! what weapon will death wear,
When he assails me? Is it knife, or sword,
A strangling cord, or sudden flaming fire?
 Brand. Neither, thou manly maid: look here, look
  here;
A cup of poison. Wherefore dost thou smile?
 Matilda. Oh God! in this the king is merciful:
My dear lov'd Huntington by poison died.
Good fellow, tell the king I thank his grace,
And do forgive his causeless cruelty.
I do forgive thee too; but do advise
Thou leave this bloody course, and seek to save
Thy soul immortal, closed in thy breast:
       [He gives it her.
Be brief, I pray you. Now, to king John's health
A full carouse:* and, God, remember not
The curse he gave himself at Robin's death,
Wishing by poison he might end his life,
If ever he solicited my love.
Farewell, good fellow. Now thy medicine works,
And with the labour, I am forc'd to rest.
 Brand. Zounds! she cares not: she makes death a jest.
 Matilda. The guiltless fear not death. Farewell,
  good friend;
I pray thee, be no trouble in my end.
     [He stands staring and quaking.
 Enter OXFORD, QUEEN, ABBESS, *Attendants.*
 Oxford And say you, Lady Abbess, that there came
One from the king unto her? what was he?
 Abbess. Yonder he stands: I know not what he is.
      [Still he stands staring.

---

 * See Mr. Gifford's note on the words *rouse* and *carouse* in his
Massinger I. 239. It would perhaps be difficult and certainly need-
less to add any thing to it.

Queen. Jesus have mercy! Oxford, come not nigh
him.

Oxford. Not nigh him, Madam? yes; keep you away.

Abbess. Come in, good Queen; I do not mean to stay.
                                [*Exit Abbess.*

Queen. Nor I to stir before I see the end.*

Oxford. Why star'st thou thus? speak fellow; answer me.
Who art thou?

Brand. A bloody villain, and a murderer!
A hundred have I slain with mine own hands.
'Twas I that starv'd the lady Bruce to death,
And her young son, at Windsor Castle late:
'Tis I have slain Matilda, blessed maid,
And now will hurry to damnation's mouth,
Forc'd by the gnawing worm of conscience. [*Runs in.*

Oxford. Hold him, for God's sake! stay the desperate
wretch.

Matilda. Oh, some good pitying man compassionate
That wretched man, so woeful desperate:
Save him for God's sake! he hath set me free
From much world's woe, much wrong, much misery.

Queen. I hear thy tongue, true perfect charity!
Chaste maid, fair maid, look up and speak to me.

Matilda. Who's here? My gracious sovereign
Isabel!
I will take strength and kneel.

Queen. Matilda sit;
I'll kneel to thee. Forgive me, gentle girl,
My most ungentle wrongs.

Matilda. Fair beauteous queen,
I give God thanks I do not think on wrongs.

Oxford. How now, Fitzwater's child! How dost thou
girl?

Matilda. Well, my good lord of Oxford; pretty well:
A little travel more, and I shall rest,

---

* " Nor I to stir before I see the end,"
belongs to the Queen, unquestionably, but the 4to. gives it to the
Abbess who has already gone out.

For I am almost at my journey's end.
Oh, that my head were raised a little up,
My drowsy head, whose dim decaying lights,
Assure me it is almost time to sleep.   [*Raise her head.*
I thank your highness; I have now some ease.
Be witness, I beseech your majesty,
That I forgive the king, with all my heart;
With all the little of my living heart,
That gives me leave to say I can forgive;
And I beseech high heaven he long may live
A happy king, a king belov'd and fear'd.
Oxford, for God's sake, to my father write
The latest commendations of his child;
And say, Matilda kept his honor's charge,
Dying a spotless maiden undefil'd.
Bid him be glad, for I am gone to joy,
I, that did turn his weal to bitter woe.
The king and he will quickly now grow friends,
And by their friendship much content will grow.
Sink earth to earth, fade flower ordain'd to fade,
But pass forth soul unto the shrine of peace;
Beg there atonement may be quickly made.
Fair queen, kind Oxford, all good you attend.
Fly forth, my soul, heaven's king be there thy friend.
                                        [*Dies.*

    Oxford. Oh pity, mourning sight!* age pitiless!
Are these the messages king John doth send?
Keep in my tears, for shame! your conduits keep,
Sad woe-beholding eyes: no, will ye not?
Why, then a God's name, weep.   [*Sit.*
    Queen. I cannot weep for wrath. Here, here! take in
The blessed body of this noble maid:

---

* The reading of the old copy is,
            " Oh *pity, mourning* sight ! age pitiless !"
and as it is just intelligible it is retained, but the sense would be
improved if we read,
            " Oh *pity-moving* sight ! age pitiless."
    Pity-moving is a common epithet, and we find it afterwards in this
play used by young Bruce,
            " My tears, my prayers, my *pity-moving* moans."

In milk white clothing let the same be laid,
Upon an open bier, that all may see
King John's untimely lust and cruelty.

[Exeunt with the body.

Oxford. I, be it so; yourself, if so you please,
Will I attend upon, and both us wait
On chaste Matilda's body, which with speed
To Windsor Castle we will hence convey.
There is another spectacle of ruth,
Old Bruce's famish'd lady and her son.

Queen. There is the king besieging of young Bruce:
His lords are there; who when they see this sight,
I know, will have small heart for John to fight.

Oxford. But where's the murderer, ha? is not he
staid?

*Servant.** Borne with a violent rage, he climb'd a
tree,
And none of us could hinder his intent;
But getting to the top boughs, fast he tied
His garters to his neck and a weak branch;
Which being unable to sustain his weight,
Down to the ground he fell, where bones and flesh
Lie pash'd† together in a pool of blood.

Oxford. Alas for woe! but this is just heaven's doom
On those that live by blood; in blood they die.
Make‡ an example of it, honest friends,
Do well, take pains, beware of cruelty.
Come, madam, come: to Windsor let us go,
And there to Bruce's grief, add greater woe.   *[Exeunt.*

---

* This servant entered probably just before Oxford's question; but
his entrance is not marked.

† To *pash*, signifies to crush or dash to pieces. So in the *Virgin
Martyr*, A. ii. sc. 2.

> With Jove's artillery, shot down at once,
> To *pash* your gods in pieces.

See Mr. Gifford's note upon this passage, and Reed's note on the
same word in *Troilus and Cressida*, A. ii. sc. 3.

‡ The 4to. has it,

> " *May* an example of it honest friends ;"

but *make* is certainly the true reading.

SCENE II.

Enter BRUCE *upon the walls.*

Bruce. Will not my bitter bannings* and sad plaints,
My just and execrable execrations,
My tears, my prayers, my pity-moving moans
Prevail, thou glorious bright lamp of the day,
To cause thee keep an obit for their souls,
And dwell one month with the Antipodes?
Bright sun, retire ; gild not this vault of death,
With thy illustrate rays: retire, retire,
And yield black night thy empery awhile :
A little while, till as my tears be spent,
My blood be likewise shed in raining drops,
By the tempestuous rage of tyrant John.
Learn of thy love, the morning : she hath wept,
Shower upon shower, of silver-dewy tears ;
High trees, low plants, and pretty little flowers
Witness her woe : on them her grief appears,
And as she drips on them, they do not let
By drop and drop their mother earth to wet.
See these hard stones, how fast small rivulets
Issue from them, though they seem issueless,
And wet-eyed woe on every thing is view'd,
Save in thy face, that smil'st at my distress.
Oh, do not drink these tears thus greedily,
Yet let the morning's mourning garment dwell
Upon the sad earth.   Wilt thou not, thou churl?
Then surfeit with thy exhalations speedily;
For all earth's venomous infecting worms
Have belch'd their several poisons on the fields,
Mixing their simples in thy compound draught.
Well, Phœbus, well, drink on, I say, drink on ;
But when thou dost ungorge thee, grant me this,
Thou pour thy poisons on the head of John.

---

* *Bannings* are *cursings*. Hundreds of examples might be added
to those collected by Steevens in a note to *King Lear*, A. ii. sc. 3. It
is a singular coincidence that *ban*, signifying a *curse*, and *ban*, a
public notice of *marriage*, should have the same origin.

Drum. Enter CHESTER, MOWBRAY, SOLDIERS, *at one*
    door : * LEICESTER, RICHMOND, *at another : soldiers.*

    Bruce. How now, my lords! were ye last night so pleas'd
With the beholding of that property,
Which John and other murderers have wrought
Upon my starved mother and her son,
That you are come again ?   Shall I again
Set open shop, shew my dead ware, dear bought
Of a relentless merchant, that doth trade
On the red sea, swoln mighty with the blood
Of noble, virtuous, harmless innocents?
Whose coal-black vessel is of ebony,
Their shrouds and tackle (wrought and wov'n by wrong)
Stretch'd with no other gale of wind, but grief,
Whose sighs with full blasts beateth on her shrouds;
The master murder is, the pilot shame,
The mariners, rape, theft, and perjury;
The burden, tyrannous oppression,
Which hourly he in England doth unlade.
Say, shall I open shop, and show my wares?

    Leicester. No, good lord Bruce, we have enough of
       that.

    Drum : Enter KING, HUBERT, SOLDIERS.

    King. To Windsor welcome, Hubert. Soft; methinks
Bruce and our lords are at a parley now?

    Bruce. Chester and Mowbray, you are John's sworn
      friends;
Will you see more? speak; answer me my lords.
I am no niggard, you shall have your fill.

    Both. We have too much, and surfeit with the woe.

    Bruce. Are you all full? there comes a ravening kite,
That both at quick, at dead, at all will smite.
He shall, he must; I, and by 'r lady, may
Command me to give over holiday,
And set wide open what you would not see.

    King. Why stand ye, lords, and see this traitor perch'd
Upon our castle's battlements so proud?
Come down young Bruce, set ope the castle gates:

---

   * The words "at one door," are necessary to make the stage
direction intelligible, but they are not found in the original.

Unto thy sov'reign let thy knee be bow'd,
And mercy shall be given to thee and thine.
   Bruce. Oh, miserable thing!
Comes mercy from the mouth of John, our king?
Why then, belike, hell will be pitiful.
I will not ope the gates, the gate I will;
The gate where thy shame, and my sorrow sits.
See my dead mother and her famish'd son!
Open thy tyrant's eyes, for to the world
I will lay open thy fell cruelties.
   King. We heard, indeed, thy mother and her son
In prison died, by wilful famishment.
   Bruce. Sin doubled upon sin! Slander'st thou the
      dead?
Unwilling willingness it shall appear,
By then I have produc'd, as I will do,
The just presumptions 'gainst your unjust act.
   King. Assail the castle, lords! alarum, drums!
And drown this screech-owl's cries with your deep
      sounds.
   Leicester. I tell thee, drummer, if thy drum thou smite,
By heav'n, I'll send thy soul to hell's dark night.
Hence with thy drum! God's passion, get thee hence!
Begone, I say; move not my patience.   [*Exit drum.*
   King. Are you advised, Leicester, what you do?
   Leicester. I am advised; for, my sovereign, know,
There's not a lord here will lift up his arm
Against the person of yon noble youth,
Till you have heard the circumstantial truth,
By good presumptions, touching this foul deed.
Therefore, go on, young Bruce; proceed, refel*
The allegation that puts in this doubt,
Whether thy mother, through her wilfulness,
Famish'd herself and her sweet son, or no.
   Bruce. Unlikely supposition: nature first denies,
That any mother, when her youngling cries,
If she have means, is so unnatural
To let it faint and starve.   But we will prove

  * This line is quoted by Steevens in a note to *Measure for Measure,*
A. v. sc. 1. to prove that the meaning of *refel* is *refute.*

She had no means, except this moanful mean,
This torture of herself.   Come forth, come forth,
Sir William Blunt, whom slander says I slew:
Come, tell the king and lords what you know true.

        Enter SIR WILLIAM BLUNT. *

  King. Thou hast betray'd our castle.

  Blunt. No: God can tell,
It was surpris'd by politic report,
And affirmation that your grace was slain.

  Richmond. Go on, Sir William Blunt:
Pass briefly to the lady's famishment,

  Blunt. About some ten days since there came one
      Brand,
Bringing a signet from my lord the king,
And this commission, signed with his hand,

               [Lords, look and read the thing.
Commanding me (as the contents express)
That I should presently deliver up
The lady Bruce and her young son to him.

  Mowbray. What time o'day was this?

  Blunt. It was, lord Mowbray, somewhat past eleven,
For we were even then sitting down to dine.

  Leicester. But did ye dine?

  Blunt. The lady and her son did not.
Brand would not stay.

  Bruce. No, Leicester, no; for here is no such sign
Of any meat's digestion.

  Richmond. But by the way, tell us I pray you, Blunt,
While she remain'd with you, was she distraught
With grief, or any other passions violent?

  Blunt. She now and then would weep, and often
      pray
For reconcilement 'twixt the king and lords.

  Chester. How to her son did she affected stand?

  Blunt. Affection could not any more affect;
Nor might a mother shew more mother's love.

  Mowbray. How to my lord the king?

---

  * In what way precisely Sir William Blunt "comes forth" does not
appear, nor is his entrance marked in the old copy.

Blunt. Oh, my Lord God!
I never knew a subject love king more.
She never would blin* telling how his grace
Sav'd her young son from soldiers and from fire;
How fair he spake, gave her her son to keep:
And then, poor lady, she would kiss her boy,
Pray for the king so hearty earnestly,
That in pure zeal she wept most bitterly.

King. I weep for her, and do by heaven protest,
I honor'd Bruce's wife, howe'er that slave
Rudely effected what I rashly will'd.
Yet when he came again, and I bethought
What bitter penance I had put them to
For my conceiv'd displeasure 'gainst old Bruce,
I bade the villain post and bear them meat:
Which he excus'd, protesting pity mov'd him
To leave wine, bread, and other powder'd meat,†
More than they twain could in a fortnight eat.

Blunt. Indeed, this can I witness with the king,
Which argues in that point his innocence:
Brand did bear in a month's provision,
But lock'd it, like a villain, far from them;
And lock'd them in a place where no man's ear
Might hear their lamentable woeful moans;
For all the issue, both of vent and light,
Came from a loover‡ at the tower's top,
Till now lord Bruce made open this wide gap.

Bruce. Had I not reason, think you, to make wide
The window, that should let so much woe forth?
Where sits my mother, martyr'd by herself,
Hoping to save her child from martyrdom;

---

* *To blin* is *to tire,* and in this sense it is met with in Spenser, and
other poets: Mr. Todd informs us that it is still in use in the north
of England. Ben Jonson in his *Sad Shepherd,* converts the verb into
a substantive, " withouten *blin.*"

† Powder'd is the old word for salted: it is in this sense Shakespeare makes Falstaff use it, when he says: " if you embowel me to
day, I'll give you leave to *powder* me and eat me to-morrow."

‡ i. e. *l'ouvert* or opening:
  Nor lighted was with window nor with *loover*
  But with continual candle light. Spenser, F. Q. b. 6.

Where stands my brother, martyr'd by himself,
Because he would not taste his mother's blood?
For thus I gather this:—my mother's teeth and chin
Are bloody with the savage cookery,
Which her soft heart, through pity of her son
Respectless, made her practise on herself;
And her right hand, with offering it the child,
Is with her own pure blood stain'd and defil'd.
My little brother's lips and chin alone
Are tainted with the blood; but his even teeth,
Like orient pearl, or snow-white ivory,
Have not one touch of blood, one little spot:
Which is an argument, the boy would not
Once stir his lips to taste that bloody food
Our cruel-gentle mother minister'd;
But as it seem'd (for see his pretty palm
Is bloody too) he cast it on the ground,
For on this side the blessed relics lie,
By famine's rage divided from this shrine.
Sad woeful mother in Jerusalem,
Who, when thy son and thou didst faint for food,
Buried his sweet flesh in thy hungry womb,
How merciless wert thou, if we compare
Thy fact and this! For my poor lady mother
Did kill herself to save my dying brother;
And thou, ungentle son of Miriam,
Why didst thou beg life when thy mother lack'd?
My little brother George did nobly act
A more courageous part: he would not eat,
Nor beg to live.   It seem'd he did not cry:
Few tears stand on his cheek, smooth is each eye;
But when he saw my mother bent to die,
He died with her. Oh, childish valiancy!
  King. Good Bruce, have done. My heart cannot con-
    tain
The grief it holds; my eyes must shower down rain.
  Leicester. Which showers are even as good,
As rain in harvest, or a swelling flood
When neighbouring meadows lack the mowers scythe.

A march for burial, with drum and fife. Enter Salisbury: Mutilda borne with nuns, one carrying a white pendant—these words writ in gold; Amoris Castitatis et Honoris Honos. The Queen following the bier, carrying a garland of flowers. Set in the midst of the stage.

Richmond. List Leicester: hear'st thou not a mournful march?

Leicester. Yes Richmond, and it seemeth old De Vere.

Oxford. Lords, by your leave, is not our sovereign here?

King. Yes, good old Aubrey.

Oxford. Ah, my gracious lord,
That you so much your high state should neglect!
Ah, God in heaven forgive this bloody deed.
Young Bruce, young Bruce, I weep
Thy mother and thy brother's wrong;
Yet to afflict thee more, more grief I bring.

Bruce. Oh, honorable Auberey de Vere,
Let sorrow in a sable suit appear:
Do not misshape her garment, like delight;
If it be grief, why cloth'st thou her in white?

Oxford. I cannot tell thee yet: I must sit down.
Attend, young Bruce, and listen to the queen;
She'll not be tongue tied: we shall have a stir
Anon, I fear, would make a man half sick.

Queen. Are you here lecher? Oh, intemperate king!
Wilt thou not see me? Come, come, shew your face,
Your grace's graceless, king's unkingly face.
What mute? hands folded, eyes fix'd on the earth?
Whose turn is next now to be murdered?
The famish'd Bruces are on yonder side,
On this another I will name anon;
One for whose head this garland I do bear,
And this fair milk-white spotless pendant too.
Look up, king John! see, yonder sits thy shame;
Yonder it lies: what, must I tell her name?
It is Matilda, poisoned by thee.

King. Matilda! oh, that foul swift-footed slave
That kills ere one have time to bid him save!
Fair gentle girl, ungently made away.
    Bruce. My banish'd uncle's daughter art thou there?
Then I defy all hope, and swear—
    Leicester. Stay, Bruce, and listen well what oath to
        swear.
Lewis the Dolphin, pitying our estate,
Is by the christian king, his father, sent
With aid to help us, and is landed too.
Lords, that will fly the den of cruelty,
And fight to free yourselves from tyranny *—
Bruce, keep that castle to the only use
Of our elected king, Lewis of France.
    Oxford. God's passion! do not so: king John is here!
Lords, whisper not with Leicester: Leicester fie!
Stir not again regardless mutiny.
Speak to them, Hugh :† I know thou lov'st the king.
Madam, go to them; nay do, for God's sake do!
Down with your stomach, for if he go down,
You must down too, and be no longer queen:
Advise you; go, entreat them speedily.
My sovereign, wherefore sit you sighing there?
The lords are all about to follow Lewis:
Up and entreat them, else they will away.
    King. Good Oxford, let them go. Why should they
        stay?
    Oxford. What, are ye desperate? That must not be.
Hear me my lords.

                    [*All stand in council.*

    King. This pendant let me see.
Amoris castitatis, et honoris honos.
She was, indeed, of love the honor once,‡

---

  * The sense is incomplete here: perhaps a line has been lost, or
Leicester suddenly recollects that Bruce has possession of Windsor
Castle, and warns him not to relinquish it.
    † An abridgment of *Hubert* apparently for the sake of the metre.
    ‡ In this line there is, in the old copy, a curious and obvious mis-
print: it stands in the 4to.—
        "She was indeed of *London* the honour once."

When she was lov'd of virtuous Huntington :
Of chastity the honor all her life ;
To impure thoughts she never could be won :
And she of honor was the honor too :
By birth, in life, she honor honored.
Bring in two tapers lighted : quick, despatch!

    Leicester. Remember, Bruce, thy charge.   Come,
        lords, away !

All but Oxford and Hubert. Away! we will away.
                 [Bring in two white tapers.

    Oxford. Hark, Leicester, but one word : a little stay.
Help me, good Hubert ! help me, gentle queen !
                          [Again confer.*

    King. How dim these tapers burn ! they give no light.
Here were two beauteous lamps, that could have taught
The sun to shine by day, the moon by night ;
But they are dim, too, clean extinguished.
Away with these, sith those fair lights be dead !

    Oxford. And, as I say, hark, Bruce, unto our talk.
Think you it is for love of England Lewis comes ?
Nay, France is not so kind ; I would it were.
Advise yourselves.   Hark, dost thou hear me, Bruce ?

    Bruce. Oxford, I do.

    Oxford. Can noble English hearts bear the French
        yoke ?
No, Leicester : Richmond, think on Lewis' sire,
That left you, and your king in Palestine.

    Queen. And think, beside, you know not Lewis' nature,
Who may be as bad as John, or, rather worse
Than he.

    Hubert. And look, my lords, upon his silent woe ;
His soul is at the door of death I know.
See, how he seeks to suck, if he could draw
Poison from dead Matilda's ashy lips.

Instead of—
        "She was indeed of *love* the honor once."
    The king is translating and commenting on the motto on the pen-
dant, as is quite evident from the manner in which he proceeds.
Besides, the measure requires a word of one syllable.

    * The lords again "stand in council" as before, while the king
fills up the interval to the audience.

I will be sworn his very heart-string nips.
A vengeance on that slave, that cursed Brand!
I'll kill him, if I live, with this right hand.

    Oxford. Thou canst not, Hubert; he hath kill'd
        himself.
But to our matter. Leicester, pray thee speak.
Young Bruce, for God's sake, let us know thy mind.

    Bruce. I would be loth to be a stranger's slave:
For England's love, I would no French king have.

    Leicester. Well Oxford, if I be deceived in John
        again,
It's long of you, lord Hubert, and the queen.
Yield up the castle, Bruce: we'll once more try
King John's proceedings. Oxford, tell him so.

        [Oxford goes to the king, does his duty, and
        talks with him.

    Bruce. I will come down. But first farewell, dear
        mother,   *[Kiss her.*
Farewell, poor little George, my pretty brother!
Now will I shut my shambles in again:
Farewell, farewell!
In everlasting bliss your sweet souls dwell.

    Oxford. But you must mend, i'faith; in faith you
        must.*

    Leicester. My lord, once more your subjects do submit,
Beseeching you to think how things have past;
And let some comfort shine on us, your friends,
Through the bright splendor of your virtuous life.

    King. I thank you all; and, Leicester, I protest,
I will be better than I yet have been.

    Bruce. Of Windsor castle here the keys I yield.

    King. Thanks Bruce: forgive me, and I pray thee see
Thy mother and thy brother buried,

        [Bruce offers to kiss Matilda.
In Windsor castle church. Do, kiss her cheek:
Weep thou on that, on this side I will weep.

    Queen. Chaste virgin, thus I crown thee with these
        flowers.

---

* This is probably addressed to the king, with whom Oxford has
been talking.

King. Let us go on to Dunmow with this maid :
Among the hallow'd nuns let her be laid.
Unto her tomb a monthly pilgrimage
Doth king John vow, in penance for this wrong.
Go forward, maids ; on with Matilda's hearse,
And on her tomb see you engrave this verse.

    Within this marble monument doth lie
    Matilda, martyr'd for her chastity.   [*Exeunt*.

EPILOGUS.

Thus is Matilda's story shown in act,
And rough hewn out by an uncunning hand :
Being of the most material points compact,
That with the certain'st state of truth do stand.

EDITION.

The Death of Robert, Earle of Huntington. Otherwise called Robin Hood of merrie Sherwodde : with the
lamentable Tragedie of chaste Matilda, his faire maid
Marian, poysoned at Dunmowe by King John. Acted
by the Right Honourable the Earle of Notingham, Lord
high Admirall of England, his servants. Imprinted at
London, for William Leake, 1601, 4to. B. L.

Also from Benediction Books ...

Wandering Between Two Worlds: Essays on Faith and Art
Anita Mathias
Benediction Books, 2007
152 pages
ISBN: 0955373700

Available from www.amazon.com, www.amazon.co.uk
www.wanderingbetweentwoworlds.com

In these wide-ranging lyrical essays, Anita Mathias writes, in lush, lovely prose, of her naughty Catholic childhood in Jamshedpur, India; her large, eccentric family in Mangalore, a sea-coast town converted by the Portuguese in the sixteenth century; her rebellion and atheism as a teenager in her Himalayan boarding school, run by German missionary nuns, St. Mary's Convent, Nainital; and her abrupt religious conversion after which she entered Mother Teresa's convent in Calcutta as a novice. Later rich, elegant essays explore the dualities of her life as a writer, mother, and Christian in the United States-- Domesticity and Art, Writing and Prayer, and the experience of being "an alien and stranger" as an immigrant in America, sensing the need for roots.

About the Author

Anita Mathias was born in India, has a B.A. and M.A. in English from Somerville College, Oxford University and an M.A. in Creative Writing from the Ohio State University. Her essays have been published in The Washington Post, The London Magazine, The Virginia Quarterly Review, Commonweal, Notre Dame Magazine, America, The Christian Century, Religion Online, The Southwest Review, Contemporary Literary Criticism, New Letters, The Journal, and two of HarperSanFrancisco's The Best Spiritual Writing anthologies. Her non-fiction has won fellowships from The National Endowment for the Arts; The Minnesota State Arts Board; The Jerome Foundation, The Vermont Studio Center; The Virginia Centre for the Creative Arts, and the First Prize for the Best General Interest Article from the Catholic Press Association of the United States and Canada. Anita has taught Creative Writing at the College of William and Mary, and now lives and writes in Oxford, England.

"Yesterday's Treasures for Today's Readers"

Titles by Benediction Classics available from Amazon.co.uk

Religio Medici, Hydriotaphia, Letter to a Friend, Thomas Browne

Pseudodoxia Epidemica: Or, Enquiries into Commonly Presumed Truths, Thomas Browne

The Maid's Tragedy, Beaumont and Fletcher

The Custom of the Country, Beaumont and Fletcher

Philaster Or Love Lies a Bleeding, Beaumont and Fletcher

A Treatise of Fishing with an Angle, Dame Juliana Berners.

Pamphilia to Amphilanthus, Lady Mary Wroth

The Compleat Angler, Izaak Walton

The Magnetic Lady, Ben Jonson

Every Man Out of His Humour, Ben Jonson

The Masque of Blacknesse. The Masque of Beauty,. Ben Jonson

The Life of St. Thomas More, William Roper

Pendennis, William Makepeace Thackeray

Salmacis and Hermaphroditus attributed to Francis Beaumont

Friar Bacon and Friar Bungay Robert Greene

Holy Wisdom, Augustine Baker

The Jew of Malta and the Massacre at Paris, Christopher Marlowe

Tamburlaine the Great, Parts 1 & 2 AND Massacre at Paris, Christopher Marlowe

All Ovids Elegies, Lucans First Booke, Dido Queene of Carthage, Hero and Leander, Christopher Marlowe

The Titan, Theodore Dreiser

Scapegoats of the Empire: The true story of the Bushveldt Carbineers, George Witton

All Hallows' Eve, Charles Williams

My Apprenticeship: Volumes I and II, Beatrice Webb

Last and First Men / Star Maker, Olaf Stapledon

Last and First Men, Olaf Stapledon

Darkness and the Light, Olaf Stapledon

The Worst Journey in the World, Apsley Cherry-Garrard

The Schoole of Abuse, Containing a Pleasaunt Invective Against Poets, Pipers, Plaiers, Iesters and Such Like Catepillers of the Commonwelth, Stephen Gosson

Russia in the Shadows, H. G. Wells

Wild Swans at Coole, W. B. Yeats

A hundreth good pointes of husbandrie, Thomas Tusser

The Collected Works of Nathanael West: "The Day of the Locust", "The Dream Life of Balso Snell", "Miss Lonelyhearts", "A Cool Million", Nathanael West

Miss Lonelyhearts & The Day of the Locust, Nathaniel West

The Worst Journey in the World, Apsley Cherry-Garrard

Scott's Last Expedition, V1, R. F. Scott

The Dream of Gerontius, John Henry Newman

The Brother of Daphne, Dornford Yates

The Poetry of Architecture: Or the Architecture of the Nations of Europe Considered in Its Association with Natural Scenery and National Character, John Ruskin

The Downfall of Robert Earl of Huntington, Anthony Munday

Clayhanger, Arnold Bennett

South: The Story of Shackleton's Last Expedition 1914-1917, Sir Ernest Shackketon

Greene's Groatsworth of Wit: Bought With a Million of Repentance, Robert Greene

Beau Sabreur, Percival Christopher Wren

The Hekatompathia, or Passionate Centurie of Love, Thomas Watson

The Art of Rhetoric, Thomas Wilson

Stepping Heavenward, Elizabeth Prentiss

Barker's Delight, or The Art of Angling, Thomas Barker
The Napoleon of Notting Hill, G.K. Chesterton

The Douay-Rheims Bible (The Challoner Revision)

Endimion - The Man in the Moone, John Lyly

Gallathea and Midas, John Lyly,

Manners, Custom and Dress During the Middle Ages and During the Renaissance Period, Paul Lacroix

Obedience of a Christian Man, William Tyndale

St. Patrick for Ireland, James Shirley

The Wrongs of Woman; Or Maria/Memoirs of the Author of a Vindication of the Rights of Woman, Mary Wollstonecraft and William Godwin

De Adhaerendo Deo. Of Cleaving to God, Albertus Magnus

Obedience of a Christian Man, William Tyndale

A Trick to Catch the Old One, Thomas Middleton

A Yorkshire Tragedy, Thomas Middleton (attrib.)

The Princely Pleasures at Kenelworth Castle, George Gascoigne

The Fair Maid of the West. Part I and Part II. Thomas Heywood

Proserpina, Volume I and Volume II. Studies of Wayside Flowers, John Ruskin

The Endeavour Journal of Sir Joseph Banks. Sir Joseph Banks

Christ Legends: And Other Stories, Selma Lagerlof; (trans. Velma Swanston Howard)

Chamber Music, James Joyce

Blurt, Master Constable, Thomas Middleton, Thomas Dekker

Since Yesterday, Frederick Lewis Allen

The Scholemaster: Or, Plaine and Perfite Way of Teachyng Children the Latin Tong , Roger Ascham

The Wonderful Year, 1603, Thomas Dekker

Waverley, Sir Walter Scott

Guy Mannering, Sir Walter Scott

Old Mortality, Sir Walter Scott

The Knight of Malta, John Fletcher

Space Prison, Tom Godwin

The Home of the Blizzard Being the Story of the Australasian Antarctic Expedition, 1911-1914, Douglas Mawson

Wild-goose Chase , John Fletcher

If You Know Not Me, You Know Nobody. Part I and Part II, Thomas Heywood

The Ragged Trousered Philanthropists, Robert Tressell

The Greater Trumps, Charles Williams

The Island of Sheep, John Buchan

Eyes of the Woods, Joseph Altsheler

The Club of Queer Trades, G. K. Chesterton

The Financier, Theodore Dreiser

Something of Myself, Rudyard Kipling

Law of Freedom in a Platform, or True Magistracy Restored, Gerrard Winstanley

Damon and Pithias, Richard Edwards

Dido Queen of Carthage: And, The Massacre at Paris, Christopher Marlowe

Cocoa and Chocolate: Their History from Plantation to Consumer, Arthur Knapp

Lady of Pleasure, James Shirley

The South Pole: An account of the Norwegian Antarctic expedition in the "Fram," 1910-12. Volume 1 and Volume 2, Roald Amundsen

A Yorkshire Tragedy, Thomas Middleton (attrib.)

The Tragedy of Soliman and Perseda, Thomas Kyd

The Rape of Lucrece. Thomas Heywood

and many others…

Tell us what you would love to see in print again, at affordable prices!
Email: **benedictionbooks@btinternet.com**